W9-BBK-543

Voting Behavior and
Presidential Elections

DATE DUE			
Mar20 7 q			

Voting Behavior & Presidential Elections

by Robert d.Cantor

Temple University

F. E. Peacock Publishers, Inc.
ITASCA, ILLINOIS 60143

Dedication

... to my Mother and the
memory of my Father

Preface

This study of the American electorate and the nature of Presidential election campaigns was made possible by the work of numerous scholars and data-gathering institutions. I am pleased to acknowledge my gratitude to those who have participated knowingly, or unknowingly, in this effort.

The data utilized were provided by the Gallup Opinion Index, the Harris Survey, and the Survey Research Center. The latter data were made available by Temple University through the Inter-university Consortium for Political Research. These data were originally collected by the Survey Research Center Political Behavior Program. Other data were provided by U.S. government publications and others doing research in this field. The interpretations of the data are the sole responsibility of the author.

I am especially indebted to those who commented on earlier drafts of the manuscript. Earl Baker, Marshall Whithed, and Murray S. Stedman, Jr., of Temple University offered advice and encouragement at the inception of this project. James S. Milne of West Chester State College and William Havard of Virginia Polytechnic Institute and State University were most helpful in the course of manuscript revisions. The cooperation of Tom LaMarre, Joyce Usher, and Gloria Reardon of F.E. Peacock Publishers, Inc. was vital in the completion of this book.

ROBERT D. CANTOR

Contents

CONTENTS (CONT'D)

1 Elections and Democracy

The right of citizens to choose their leaders is the cornerstone of democratic government. Presidential elections offer the individual an effective opportunity to register his support for an incumbent leader or indicate his preference for change. In the hands of the democratic citizen, the ballot is the most potent weapon for ensuring responsive government. In turn, the responsiveness of government determines the degree of legitimacy it is accorded by the people.

The Jeffersonian notion of direct participatory democracy through the forum of the town meeting may be appealing, but it is impractical in modern society. Indeed, it was unrealistic at the time of the American Revolution. The framers of the Constitution were faced with the problem of providing for popular participation in government without limiting the ability of elected representatives to govern effectively.

The roles and rights of the new American citizen were best set forth in *The Federalist*. This set of essays, written by James Madison, John Jay, and Alexander Hamilton, constituted an eloquent argument for the rationale that produced the Constitution.[1] In Federalist 10, Madison dealt with the problem of maintaining democratic government in a nation too large for the Jeffersonian concept of direct citizen participation:

The two great points of difference between a democracy and a republic are: first, the delegation of the government, in the latter, to a small number of citizens elected by the rest; secondly, the greater number of citizens, and greater sphere of country, over which the latter may be extended.

The effect of the first difference is, on the one hand, to refine and enlarge the public views, by passing them through the medium of a chosen body of citizens, whose wisdom may best discern the true interest of their country, and whose patriotism and love of justice will be least likely to sacrifice it to temporary or partial considerations.[2]

Madison assumed that elected representatives would act in the best interests of the nation. The government of the United States is clearly not based upon the principle of majority rule in terms of decision making or legislative function. Rather, the majority expresses itself in elections by choosing their legislators and their President.

The focus of this book is voting behavior in Presidential elections, which represents the form of political participation that attracts the largest percentage of the citizenry. Presidential elections are salient to most people because they involve issues and personalities that receive intensive media coverage. The effectiveness of these contests in assuring responsive national leadership is a measure of whether or not the political system is working as intended by the Founding Fathers.

Watergate

The Watergate affair has brought the legitimacy of our political institutions, especially the Presidency, into question. The Watergate break-in and subsequent disclosures of illegality and impropriety by those in the administration reflect an insensitivity to the nature of the relationship between the President and the citizenry. It is imperative that the democratic citizen view his government as responsive, and violations of the public trust diminish the legitimacy of the democratic process.

In a real sense Watergate is a symptom of the enormous

increase in Presidential power since 1932. It is the culmination of an implicit assumption that accountability to the electorate is important only in terms of retaining sufficient support to win reelection. While the Founding Fathers recognized the impracticality of direct citizen participation in government, they did not intend Presidential elections to represent a mandate for four years of unlimited Presidential power. The trauma of Watergate underscores the vital link Presidential elections represent between the government and the citizens of the United States.

Fundamental questions are raised about the very nature of our political system. Do Presidential elections afford the people a periodic review of their government? Are voters sufficiently rational or knowledgeable to make voting more than a democratic love feast? The answers to these questions require an understanding of the forces which shape the individual voting decision.

VALUES, ATTITUDES, OPINIONS

Voting in Presidential elections does not take place in a vacuum. The choice an individual expresses is a reflection of both opinions on contemporary issues and deep-rooted beliefs that comprise his value system. The value system includes general notions of acceptability and unacceptability—or right and wrong—which remain constant over a long period of time. Constancy of value systems, however, does not guarantee internal consistency. Certain of an individual's values may be in conflict with other values he holds. He may subscribe to man's equality before God, for example, but this value may be in conflict with his deep-seated racial prejudice.

Within the broad context of his own value system the individual develops attitudes toward a myriad of objects or situations. These attitudes formed within the parameters of a value system are enduring and reflect psychological predispositions toward events or situations that have occurred or might occur in the future.[3]

Opinions are formed around objects or events that have raised a question. The voter's choice in elections represents the expression of an opinion because he is offered an alternative. The catalyst for the formation of individual and public opinion is conflict, which raises issues to the point of general interest and encourages people to take sides. Opinions are more subject to change than are attitudes because of the controversy surrounding them. Conscious efforts to influence opinion are made by proponents and opponents of any policy or candidate. The mere existence of conflict, however, does not ensure the degree of involvement necessary for an individual to form an opinion.[4] For conflict to serve as an opinion catalyst, the issues must have some salience. The debate over building the Alaskan pipeline reached the point of salience in late 1973 because of the energy crisis. Before that time it is unlikely that more than a small percentage of the public was aware of the controversy or had an opinion concerning it.

Individual opinion is not the concrete expression of well-reasoned thought that is implied by the polls. The aggregate data include those of both deep and weak conviction, those who are well-informed, and those with little knowledge and less concern. The input that creates informed opinions is a function of clues that individuals receive from sources in society as well as their psychological predispositions. Alexis de Tocqueville put it well:

> If every man had to prove for himself all the truths of which he makes use every day, he would never come to an end of it. He would wear himself out proving preliminary points and make no progress. Since life is too short for such a course and human faculties are too limited, man has to accept as certain a whole heap of facts and opinions which he has neither the leisure nor power to examine and verify for himself, things which cleverer men than he have discovered and which the crowd accepts. On that foundation he then builds the house of his own thoughts.[5]

This observation, written in the early 1800s, is even more pertinent today. The complexity of contemporary political life compels the individual to rely on political information gleaned from the media, peer groups, and political parties as the basis for "the house of his own thoughts." Individuals are exposed to a myriad of issues, principally through the media, but only those that are perceived as relevant will be accorded the attentiveness that can result in knowledge.[6] Very few issues will strike an individual as sufficiently salient to impel increased awareness. Public affairs are not the most important facet in the lives of most Americans, and information does not, in itself, lead to the formation of opinions on political matters. The individual must have a conceptual framework within which the information can be synthesized and applied to the political world. At this point, according to Leo Bogart, "he is ready to do a little political thinking."[7]

One important facet of individual opinions has been referred to as the "action component." This is recognition that some attitudes toward political objects are more likely to be accompanied by relevant action than others.[8] Polls showing the relative strength of Presidential candidates are taken seriously because elections are structured situations in which everyone knows the rules.[9] Voters are aware that their vote may aid in the election of a candidate they favor—or the defeat of one they oppose.

A problem in interpreting polls is that many shades of opinion are obscured by questions which require a stated preference of Presidential candidates. Such polls indicate the direction of opinion but not the intensity of it. It is the intensity which plays a large part in the determination of whether or not the opinion will remain constant throughout the election campaign and whether the opinion will be followed up in voting. Intensity is not synonymous with concern or interest, although it is often interpreted in this manner. The concerned citizen will be apt to develop strong opinions about issues and candidates. The intensity of this individual's opinions is of great importance because the concerned citizen is most likely to translate his opinion into his vote.

But intensity of opinion is not the sole purview of those most interested in the political milieu. Measures of intensity may actually be reflections of individual personality traits rather than reactions to the specific issue at hand. Individuals who react strongly to outside stimuli will also be prone to express great intensity of feeling on most questions, although this intensity may not be accompanied by concern or even interest.[10] Personality traits may also affect the direction of opinion. Some individuals are apt to be negative, while others will more than likely give positive responses.[11] These uncertainties are inherent in the study of human attitudes and should not be used as a reason to avoid pursuit of the role of opinion in voting behavior.

RATIONALITY

The rationality or irrationality of the American voter is of considerable importance in consideration of voting behavior. If most voters are rational, Presidential elections will fulfill their promise of being periodic reviews of government performance. If voters cast their ballots for largely irrational reasons, Presidential elections will take on the hue of a public relations contest between advertising agencies, with the White House as first prize.

There are two basic questions in the consideration of rationality in voting behavior: First, how do we define rational thinking and action in the context of man's relation to political society? Second, under what circumstances is voting behavior most likely to conform to our conception of rationality?

There are many definitions of rationality. The common thread is the idea of seeking the most appropriate means to reach the desired end. The following definition is applicable to political man:

> Rationality . . . involves recourse to certain intellectual procedures in an interpretive but essentially practical encounter with some given situation, with the procedures selected being said to be recognizable as implicit in the very fact of the encounter itself, when full consciousness of the situation is attained.[12]

The use of intellectual procedures raises rationality above the level of a gut reaction. Rational voting decisions, then, are those that are made after contemplation of the facts and the viable alternatives. Rational means selected to reach desirable ends are those which appear well suited to the task on the basis of experience or knowledge. Presidential elections offer the voter alternatives in the form of candidates, issues, and political parties. The rationality of voter perceptions of these alternatives determines the rationality of the voting decision.

There are an infinite number of points on the scale between rationality and irrationality. Individuals are more rational in their opinions when the subject matter is relevant and closely associated with individual action. Voting is the political act most closely associated with opinion. In *The Responsible Electorate,* V. O. Key, Jr., places the question of rationality in perspective:

> The perverse and unorthodox argument of this little book is that voters are not fools. To be sure, many individual voters act in odd ways indeed; yet in the large the electorate behaves about as rationally as we should expect, given the clarity of the alternatives presented to it, and the character of the information available to it.[13]

The latter part of this passage casts light on one of the major handicaps in the development of rational opinion. Ambiguous alternatives and contradictory information are not pathways to rational judgments. Even those individuals who possess the interest and political perceptivity that are requisite for recognizing the best means to the desired ends may be misled by lack of information. The Presidential election of 1964, in which Lyndon B. Johnson won reelection by a landslide, is a case in point. Johnson's avowed desire to avoid raising the degree of American involvement in Vietnam, contrasted to Barry Goldwater's hawkish attitudes, materially aided Johnson's campaign. Few individuals outside of Johnson's inner circle could have foreseen the escalation of the war that followed the election.

Presidential elections can be considered an effective instrument in the democratic process only if voters reach their decisions after rational reflection on the key elements in the campaign. In this sense, reflection indicates an awareness of capabilities of the respective candidates and at least a general notion of the foremost issues. Without the minimal level of knowledge implicit in this framework, the voter might flip a coin to arrive at a decision. There is another factor, however, that influences the electorate — political parties command the loyalty of some voters and may serve as an adequate reference point for the party faithful. The fact that the Democratic or Republican Party has nominated a particular candidate may be sufficient reason for some to support him. The loyalist may also have sufficient faith in his party to believe that any issue positions adopted by the organization are appropriate. Thus the alternatives in issues, candidates, and parties must be considered by the voter in forming a rational voting decision. These three factors can also be used as reference points in our study of voting behavior in Presidential elections.[14]

ISSUES

It is obvious that for an issue to be a factor in a Presidential election it must be perceived in partisan terms by a substantial segment of the electorate. This may mean that the voter recognizes that the candidates have taken different stances on a given problem. Or it may reflect the voter's assessment of which party or candidate is best equipped to handle a problem that may loom in the future, such as economic recession.

One question that should be considered in a discussion of the impact of issues on voting decisions is how important a particular issue is and to how many people. Because school busing to achieve racial integration is an issue that affects many voters, it is important in an election campaign. The proposed closing of a particular military base, however, is an issue only to those in the immediate area who will feel the effects of the closing. Another question is the meaningfulness of the popular sentiment expressed in public opinion polls on a variety of issues. If the opinions represent intense feelings they may well influence the voting decision, but if they are offhand responses to issues not viewed as pertinent the polls may be misleading. Also of concern is whether a particular issue is viewed in partisan terms by the voter. If it is not so viewed, there will be little impact on the voting decision. If it is, the extent to which opinion on the issue is influenced by positions taken by candidates or parties must be considered. These are some of the facets to be considered in a discussion of the relationship between issues and voting decisions in Presidential elections.

CANDIDATES

"I vote for the man, not the party" is an oft-repeated phrase in discussions of Presidential elections. There are two interesting elements in consideration of the candidate's effect on the voting decision. First, do voters form judgments of candidates independent of party affiliation? Second, what are the attributes of Presidential candidates that are most important to the electorate?

Since the election of the personable John F. Kennedy in 1960, charisma has become a key word in discussing Presidential hopefuls. We cannot, however, be certain that this was the deciding factor in 1960. Neither Richard M. Nixon nor Lyndon B. Johnson fit the mold of a public relations man's ideal candidate, and yet the former won twice and latter once in a landslide. The other personal attribute thought to be important in the success of Presidential candidates is the appearance of competence. Both Nixon and Johnson based their campaigns on a wealth of government experience. The relative influence of charisma and the appearance of competence is an interesting question. If it is assumed that the man is more important than the party, one of these factors will likely determine the voting decision. But if the position that most voters pick the party is taken, it is likely that perceptions of the candidate are brought into line with the decision to vote for a particular party.

PARTIES

The view that party loyalty is the most important element in shaping voting decisions in Presidential elections is a widely accepted tenet of voting behavior.[15] This is largely due to the stability of the two-party system and the inability of third parties to endure, let alone elect a President. The Democratic and Republican parties are institutions to which most Americans are believed to have some degree of allegiance.

Important questions arise in consideration of the pervasiveness of party loyalty in Presidential elections. If the idea that most voters have an emotional attachment to one party is accepted, can this be translated into voting behavior? To what extent does party loyalty determine a voter's perceptions of key issues or candidate competence? This leads to the basic question: In Presidential elections, what percentage of the electorate is likely to vote for candidates of a different party than they have customarily supported?

This brief introduction to the study of voting behavior has attempted to provide a perspective of the role of Presidential elections in the American political system. The formation of political opinions has been discussed briefly, along with the principal objects of opinion in Presidential elections—issues, candidates, and parties. Many questions have been raised. Hopefully, the chapters that follow will cast light on these questions and lead to a better understanding of the complexities of voting behavior.

NOTES

1. *The Federalist* is probably the outstanding American contribution to political theory concerning constitutional government and a federal system. See Gottfried Dietze, *The Federalist* (Baltimore: Johns Hopkins Press, 1960) for an excellent discussion of the Federalist papers.

2. All of the Federalist papers were signed "Publius." No. 10 is credited to James Madison.

3. See James J. Best, *Public Opinion: Micro and Macro* (Homewood, Ill.: Dorsey Press, 1973), especially Chap. 1 for an excellent discussion of the formation of what Best calls the "perceptual screen."

4. Philip E. Converse, "The Nature of Belief Systems in Mass Publics," in David Apter, ed., *Ideology and Discontent* (New York: Free Press, 1964), p. 251.

5. Alexis de Tocqueville, *Democracy in America*, edited by J. P. Mayer (New York: Doubleday & Co., 1969), p. 434.

6. Leo Bogart, *Silent Politics: Polls and the Awareness of Public Opinion* (New York: John Wiley & Sons, 1972), p. 99.

7. Ibid., p. 2.

8. Daniel Katz, "The Functional Approach to the Study of Attitudes," William J. Crotty, ed., in *Public Opinion and Politics* (New York: Holt, Rinehart & Winston, 1970), p. 295.

9. Irving Crespi, "What Kind of Attitude Measures Are Predictive of Behavior?" *Public Opinion Quarterly*, Fall 1971, p. 334.

10. Robert E. Lane and David O. Sears, *Public Opinion* (Englewood Cliffs, N.J.: Prentice-Hall, 1964), pp. 7–9.

11. See Robert E. Agger, "Independents and Party Identifiers: Characteristics and Behavior in 1952," in Eugene Burdick and Arthur J. Brodbeck, eds., *American Voting Behavior* (Glencoe, Ill.: Free Press, 1959) for an excellent discussion of this point.

12. David Kettler, "Political Science and Political Rationality," in David Spitz, ed., *Political Theory and Social Change* (New York: Atherton Press, 1967), pp. 75–76.

13. V. O. Key, Jr., with Milton C. Cummings, *The Responsible Electorate* (New York: Vintage Books, 1968), p. 7.

14. The use of parties, candidates, and issues as key variables stems from Angus Campbell, Gerald Gurin, and Warren E. Miller, *The Voter Decides* (Evanston, Ill.: Row, Peterson & Co., 1954).

15. See Angus Campbell, Philip E. Converse, Warren E. Miller, and Donald E. Stokes, *The American Voter* (New York: John Wiley & Sons, 1960), especially Chap. 6.

2 Presidential Elections: Theory and Classification

The shifting political power balance which revolves about electoral contests for the Presidency can be a source of never-ending fascination. Despite the myriad data available about Presidential elections and continuous scrutiny of the national political scene, events occur which make yesterday's predictions today's errors of judgment.

A brief review of the career of Richard M. Nixon since his defeat by John F. Kennedy in 1960 illustrates this point. Nixon ran for governor of California in 1962 in an effort to remain a viable national political figure. When he was defeated, political pundits agreed that this race was his last hurrah. After the landslide victory of Lyndon B. Johnson in 1964, most observers wrote off the Republican Party as a Presidential threat for periods ranging from a decade to a century. But the conventional wisdom of political experts was wrong, and the Republicans elected their Presidential candidate in 1968—Richard M. Nixon. Finally, in a bitter climax to a stormy political career, Nixon was forced to resign in 1974.

Thus a candidate written off as a has-been in 1962 and a party

12

regarded as impotent in 1964 teamed up to win in 1968. Then, in 1972, Nixon's reelection compared to Johnson's 1964 victory in scope. As the Watergate scandal began to emerge from the shadows in the months following this election, innuendos gave way to thorough investigation which brought indictment and sentencing of key administration figures. The message is clear—Democrats and Republicans alike compete for the Presidency against a background of events that are impossible to foresee and difficult to assess in terms of their political impact.

Theories that attempt to explain past and predict future trends in Presidential elections have one common idea: They are all based on the notion of voter loyalty to the Democratic or Republican Party. This link of individual with party is believed to endure over time and to be deflected only by unusual political events. The theories differ in the explanations they offer for party loyalty. An examination of the more prominent theories can provide a framework for a better understanding of Presidential elections. There are three principal approaches. First, some theorists look to broad political trends for an explanation of party alignment. Second, some scholars view psychological predispositions as the force which dominates electoral decision making. Third, there are students of voting behavior who believe sociological factors determine the party affiliation of most citizens.

POLITICAL TRENDS

The argument has been advanced that one party is likely to dominate Presidential elections for decades by successfully building a coalition of various groups and interests that represent the predominant political trends of the era.[1] The prolonged Democratic rule in the 1932–52 period encouraged this view. Coalition building based on broad secular trends is dependent on the existence of large-scale bloc voting. These blocs may be built on ethnic, economic, racial, or geographic considerations of sufficient impact to attract large numbers of citizens who identify strongly with the group. They extend this loyalty to the party which appears to represent group interests and concerns best.

In *The Emerging Republican Majority*, Kevin Phillips looks to geographically based but ethnically and racially inspired cleavages to explain voting shifts. These realignments are caused by the introduction of a new element in the cultural mix of the nation.

> Ethnic polarization is a longstanding hallmark of American politics, not an unprecedented and menacing development—ethnic and cultural division has so often shaped American politics that, given the immense midcentury impact of Negro enfranchisement and integration, reaction to this change almost inevitably had to result in political realignment. Moreover, American history has another example of a persecuted minority—the Nineteenth-Century Irish—who, in the face of considerable discrimination and old-stock animosity, likewise poured their ethnic numbers into the Democratic Party alone. . . .[2]

Phillips, who was active in Nixon's 1968 campaign as an aide to John Mitchell, considers periods of one-party domination the norm for American politics. It is the "obsolescence of the prevailing ideology or impetus of the dominant party"[3] that leads to change in party control of the White House. Phillips points to the inability of Democratic administrations to cope with the "Negro socioeconomic revolution" as the harbinger of an era of Republican rule. In his analysis of the 1968 Presidential election, he considers the Nixon and Wallace vote—about 57 percent—as anti-Democratic votes and predicts the movement of Wallace supporters to the Republican Party. The results of the 1972 election would add credence to his argument if the notion that periods of one-party domination are likely to continue to be the norm in American politics is accepted.

Several assumptions are implicit in Phillips's theory. The formation of voting blocs is predicated upon the belief that specific issues are of long-term concern to the electorate. This proposition will be examined later in the book. There is also an assumption that the minority party—in this instance the Democrats—will continue to adopt positions that alienate the majority of the electorate. Politicians are not fools, and either party may be expected to adjust its policies to political realities. The broad-based constituencies of American parties and the obvious profit in espousing centrist positions make it unlikely that either Democrats or Republicans would willingly forfeit the opportunity for success in Presidential elections because of political ideology. Phillips also looks to the population migration to historically Republican areas (such as the Sun Belt) as evidence that a period of Republican ascendancy has commenced. His assumption that voters adopt the policies of their new surroundings is tenuous at best, however. One need only observe the increasing Democratic vote in formerly Republican suburbs of many large cities to cite an example of the tendency of voters to take their politics with them.

The thrust of Phillips's argument is that ethnic, racial, and geographic alignments are the dominant force in American Presidential politics, and one party will be the beneficiary for extended periods of time. Political trends may also be short term as opposed to the long-term characteristics Phillips emphasized. V. O. Key, Jr., stressed the importance of short-term trends in *The Responsible Electorate*.[4] Key's analysis of Presidential elections from 1932 to 1960 is a refreshing departure from the conclusions of many voting behavior observers who place great weight on the ability of the media to manipulate the American voter.[5] Key notes that:

> In American presidential campaigns of recent decades the portrait of the American electorate that develops from the data is not one of an electorate straitjacketed by social determinants or moved by subconscious urges triggered by devilishly skillful propagandists. It is rather one of an electorate moved by concern about central and relevant questions of public policy, of governmental performance, and of executive personality.[6]

Key endorses the idea that voting for Presidential candidates is predicated more on negative than on positive factors. The electorate votes against rather than for a party or candidate.[7] This is important for democratic theory because, if this view is accurate, Presidential elections do function as periodic reviews of government performance. According to Key, the failure of the Republican Party to elect a President in the 1932–52 period was due to the fact that the voters were generally satisfied by the policies of the Democratic regime.[8]

The importance of Key's work is the emphasis it places upon the necessity for the President to be responsive to the electorate if he is to remain in office. Key regards party loyalty as a strong factor in the individual's voting decision. The more loyal is a partisan, the more likely he is to resist any pull that might cause him to vote for the Presidential candidate of the other party.[9] *The Responsible Electorate* is a blend of theory based on short-term political trends and psychological predispositions, namely, party identification.[10]

PSYCHOLOGICAL THEORY

The pervasiveness of psychological factors in Presidential voting behavior is probably the most widely accepted premise. An individual's perceptions of his political milieu are believed to be largely shaped by psychological predispositions. This notion springs from the idea that an individual is politicized by his early environment. Psychological theorists believe these influences lead to long-term emotional ties to one of the principal objects in the political world, the party. The party is seen as the arbiter in political affairs, and its stand on issues and its selection of candidates are believed to have a profound influence on voters who identify with the Democratic or Republican party.

Angus Campbell, Gerald Gurin, and Warren E. Miller led the way to placing increased emphasis on the importance of psychological factors in *The Voter Decides*, a study based on the 1952 Presidential election. The major hypothesis of this book is that more than one factor is involved in an individual's voting decision, and the probability of a voter acting in a specific manner is in proportion to the number of positive factors influencing him.[11] In the search for explanation of voting behavior in Presidential elections, three major psychological variables are established: party identification, issue orientation, and candidate orientation.

The authors of *The Voter Decides* establish party identification as the most important of these variables, although it is recognized that they interact with one another.

> The present analysis of party identification is based on the assumption that the two parties serve as standard-setting groups for a significant proportion of the people of this country. In other words, it is assumed that many people associate themselves psychologically with one or the other of the parties, and that this identification has predictable relationships with their perceptions, evaluation, and actions.[12]

Party affiliation is established by self-identification. Gradations of degree of affiliation are established for Democrats and Republicans, while those who refuse to claim even a weak partisanship are classed as independents. Their voting behavior was not considered as a criterion of classification by Campbell et al., who rest upon the assumption that "party identification is a psychological force with important relations to political behavior—these self-classifications must imply something more than a capricious choice of proffered labels at the time of interview."[13] Later, the same book notes: "Our concept of party identification leads us to assume that a person who associates himself strongly with a party will conform to what he sees to be party standards and will support party goals."[14] Group influences are relegated to a minor niche compared with the psychological roots of an individual's partisanship.

The most comprehensive survey research study of the characteristics of the country's voters is another work with Angus Campbell as the primary author. *The American Voter* by Angus Campbell, Philip E. Converse, Warren E. Miller, and Donald E. Stokes covers both the 1952 and 1956 Presidential elections through the medium of interviews with different samples of the electorate in which sufficiently similar questions were asked to allow comparison. The authors of this work see the value of survey research in the study of voting behavior as permitting an analysis of the determinants of an individual's motivation.[15] This marks a trend away from interpreting elections simply by utilizing breakdowns of precinct or division election returns. The authors outline their intent as follows:

> Our hypothesis is that the partisan choice the individual voter makes depends in an immediate sense on the strength and direction of the elements comprising a field of psychological forces, where these elements are interpreted as attitudes toward the perceived objects of national politics. Measurements of the direction and intensity of these attitudes can be used to account for the behavior of most voters and hence to confirm our theoretical hypothesis.[16]

Thus they see voting behavior as a resultant of psychological forces. Their conception of identification with party "as a factor that is normally antecedent to these forces, yet susceptible at times to change by them" is a logical development of this concept.

The notion of the "funnel of causality" is introduced as the theoretical framework for *The American Voter*. All variables that might influence the individual's voting decision are considered as occurring in a time sequence that moves toward the narrow end of the funnel. As events approach this end, they are seen as "more completely relevant, personal, and political."[17]

Events which are not intrinsically political may become part of an individual's political awareness through his own translation of the event. If a voter perceives a recent layoff, for example, in political terms, this becomes an element in his voting decision. If on the other hand he sees no connection between his job situation and the choice of a President, the same event is nonpolitical. This approach is primarily concerned with political attitudes close to the time of voting decision. Since this is the narrow end of the funnel, a minimum number of variables needs to be considered at this time. It is crucial to this concept, however, to appreciate the relationship of the variables proximate to the voting decision with events further back in the funnel. As Campbell et al. see it, "the field at the present moment is seen as a product of the field in the immediate neighborhood at a time just past."[18]

The American Voter utilizes the same basic research strategy developed for *The Voter Decides,* with fuller amplification. In *The American Voter,* the long-run effects of psychological forces on the ultimate voting decision are explored. In the author's words,

> . . . we want a set of empirical relationships that carry us deeper into the funnel, and move outward from events and attitudes that are expressly political. We want to explore the political core of the funnel, particularly within the chain of personal events, at a considerable distance from the current vote.[19]

The personal events considered most relevant in this study are those that contribute to the individual's party self-identification. For this reason the authors "begin our search for causality at the psychological level and conceive of the voting act as the resultant of attitudinal forces."[20] Party identification is established in this work in the same manner as in *The Voter Decides.* The index established depends on self-identification with one of seven classifications of voters.[21] Both the construct of this index and the interpretations of the authors are the keys to this study. The authors note that

> Apparently party has a profound influence across the full range of political objects to which the individual voter responds. The strength of relationship between party identification and the dimensions of partisan attitude suggests that responses to each element of national politics are deeply affected by the individual's enduring party attachments.[22]

An interesting distinction is drawn between the psychological approach, which uses attitudinal materials, and the sociological approach, which is dependent upon demographic factors. The authors of this study believe that the latter

> . . . have no political significance save that which may be brought to them by the discovery of relationships between them and political behaviors. It follows from the fact of remoteness that these concepts tend to account for much less variance than do attitudinal materials drawn closer to the behavior.[23]

The American Voter thus continues in the same vein as *The Voter Decides,* but with greatly expanded areas of interest. It also has the advantage of comparative surveys over the span of two elections. Both works place party identification at the top of the list of factors influencing voting behavior in Presidential elections. This raises a significant question: Does an individual's stated party tie refer to local, state, or national party organizations, or does it apply to all levels of party activity? This question will be dealt with in the next chapter. Regardless, the notion of enduring party loyalty is at the heart of psychological theories of voting behavior.

SOCIOLOGICAL THEORY

Sociological influences on voting behavior include such factors as economic status, education, ethnicity, and group membership. These influences are believed to mold the perceptions of a voter in a manner that will endure over time. The underlying premise is that each individual identifies with a group or groups; and this affinity encourages the individual to adopt the political perceptions of the group.

In the first sociologically oriented survey research project concerned with voting behavior, *The People's Choice* by Paul Lazarsfeld, Bernard Berelson, and Hazel Gaudet, an attempt was made to trace the development of the voting decision. The study was conducted in Erie County, Ohio, during the 1940 Presidential campaign. The thrust of this study was to discover *why* people voted as they did (or didn't), as opposed to *how* they voted. In this respect *The People's Choice* represents a breakthrough in voting behavior research.[24]

The authors studied the types of voters whose voting decision changed during the campaign and concluded: "The notion that the people who switch parties during the campaign are mainly the reasoned, thoughtful, conscientious people who were convinced by the issues of the election is just plain wrong."[25] Party preference was measured by the stated vote intention before or during the campaign, rather than stable preference over the time span of several elections. It is suggested that the effect of the campaign "activated the indifferent, reinforced the partisan, and converted the doubtful."[26] Their efforts to answer the question of with which group the respondents were most likely to vote used this approach:

> The approximate procedure will be to select a sample of people and to take an inventory of the groups they belong to. There will be the family, co-workers, family associates, neighbors and groups of people 'they go with.' For each respondent we shall need a list of the people who form these groups and their vote intentions. As the first result we will have a measure of political homogeneity of the different types of groups.[27]

This emphasis on the importance of group voting is based on the underlying assumption that group membership is unlikely to change over time. This view has not gone unchallenged. Campbell, Gurin, and Miller, for example, note that "Many a political prognosticator has been led into difficulties by the confident assumption that the major population classes will vote in the next election as they have voted in the recent past."[28] They found that this assumption was particularly inept in 1952.

This rebuttal to one of the key premises of sociological theories about voting behavior highlights one of the major areas of disagreement between the sociological and psychological theorists. The authors of *The People's Choice* proceed from "the underlying social structure variables," while those of *The Voter Decides* "postulated the independence of attitude structures from social structures."[29]

Voting by Bernard R. Berelson, Paul F. Lazarsfeld, and William McPhee is a study of voting behavior in Elmira, New York, during the 1948 Presidential campaign. As in *The People's Choice*, potential voters were asked about their voting intention. The book's conclusions are based upon their ultimate voting decisions. *Voting* concludes that "Stability in vote is characteristic of those interested and instability of those not particularly interested."[30] The small percentage of party changers between elections is noted, and it is concluded that those whose change may decide close elections are "disproportionately located among those closer to the border line of disinterest."[31]

Berelson et al. refer to the democratic "ideal" political man as a highly interested nonpartisan. Since there is a strong correlation between partisanship and interest in this study, they conclude that the independent "of high interest but low partisanship is a deviant case."[32] This proposition will be examined later.

The emphasis on the importance of group voting behavior is similar to that in *The People's Choice*. In *Voting*, the authors maintain that

> The solid foundations of American political parties are in distinctive social groups that not only have "interests" involved but have sufficient social differentiation from other groups, sufficient continuity between generations, and sufficient closed or in-group contact in successive generations to transform these initial political interests into persistent and durable social traditions. It is the re-emergence of these traditions, as much as fresh political developments, that characterizes a modern political campaign.[33]

Emphasis on sociological determinants of voting behavior in Presidential elections is predicated on the idea of long-range attachment of individuals to groups which serve as political points of reference. Politics based on this type of arrangement would encompass parties consisting of well-defined groups of voters whose loyalty to the group would be transferred to the party with which the group aligns itself. The durable nature of the voter's attachments would result in stable party strength. This, in turn, would inevitably lead to the domination of Presidential elections by one party for extended periods of time. This theory of group voting is somewhat similar to that of Kevin Phillips discussed earlier in this chapter. Phillips's dependence on the importance of voting blocs implicitly assumes that individuals are tied to the group by sociological factors.

The voting studies cited in this chapter represent the basic approaches to developing an understanding of the dynamics of voting behavior in Presidential elections. All of the theories place great weight on the underlying stability of voter allegiance to one party. We shall have an opportunity to compare theory to political reality as we explore the relationship between key theoretical variables and voting behavior.

CLASSIFICATION OF ELECTIONS

It is obvious that some voters do change their party vote in Presidential elections. The impact — or lack of impact — of these changes on long-term party alignment is a subject of interest. Classifications of elections have been developed that interpret the influence of party loyalty on Presidential elections.

Philip E. Converse introduced the concept of a "normal vote." This idea rests on the premise that party loyalty is stable over the long term but may be altered by other factors in any given Presidential election. The probability of a voter casting a ballot for the candidate of the other party is described as "a simple function of the strength of felt loyalty."[34] The other basic consideration in establishing the parameters of the normal vote is voter turnout. Elections are decided by the segment of the electorate that votes, and study of data from past elections demonstrates that some individuals are consistently more likely to vote than others.[35] The normal division of the vote in Presidential elections, therefore, is derived from consideration of party identification and turnout. Presidential elections can be categorized by classifying the deviations from the normal vote. The classifications are based on the expectation of the nature of the deviation — long or short term.

Angus Campbell classifies elections as maintaining, deviating, or realigning.[36] In maintaining elections, the "pattern of partisan attachments prevailing in the preceding period persists, and the majority party wins the Presidency."[37] The election of John F. Kennedy in 1960 is considered as maintaining because the candidate of the majority party was victorious.

Deviating elections are those in which "the basic division of party loyalties is not seriously disturbed, but the influence of short-term forces on the vote is such that it brings about the defeat of the majority party."[38] Deviating elections are marked by higher turnouts than maintaining elections. It is the presence of short-term forces that stimulates an increase in voter turnout and brings those without strong party attachments to the polls. This, according to Campbell, increases the possibility of deviation from the normal vote. Dwight D. Eisenhower's victories in 1952 and 1956 are examples of deviating elections, as they accomplished the defeat of the majority Democratic Party.

The third type of election identified by Campbell, the realigning election,[39] is marked by change of the underlying partisanship in sufficiently large numbers of voters to create a new majority party. The political upheaval which accompanied the depression of the 1930s and Franklin D. Roosevelt's ascendancy to power is the best recent example. Realigning elections are marked by grave national problems which divide the electorate along new lines.

The theories of voting behavior and classifications of Presidential elections presented in this chapter provide a framework within which we can examine the forces that are important in shaping the individual's voting decision. They also offer reference points to use in considering the significance and meaning of Presidential elections. Since 1952 the Presidency has changed party every eight years. Can this fact be reconciled with the theories presented in this chapter? Is the assumption of stable party loyalty on which the classifications of elections are based warranted? What other explanations of voting behavior in Presidential elections are appropriate? The following chapters will cast light on these questions and, undoubtedly, raise new ones.

NOTES

1. See V. O. Key, Jr., "Secular Realignment and the Party System," *Journal of Politics*, No. 2, Vol. 21, May 1959, pp. 198–210. Another important work that emphasizes the importance of political trends is Walter Dean Burnham, *Critical Elections and the Mainsprings of American Politics* (New York: W. W. Norton Co., 1970). Burnham sees the failure of government to react to demands of the electorate as the catalyst for political realignment.

An excellent discussion of the theories of Kevin Phillips (*The Emerging Republican Majority*) and Walter Dean Burnham (*Critical Elections and the Mainsprings of American Politics*) is found in Douglas Price, "Critical Elections and Party History: A Critical View," *Polity*, Vol. 4, No. 2 (Winter 1971), pp. 236–42.

2. Kevin Phillips, *The Emerging Republican Majority* (New York: Arlington House, 1969), p. 470. Phillips's thesis is challenged effectively in Nelson W. Polsby and Aaron B. Wildavsky, *Presidential Elections*, 3rd ed. (New York: Charles Scribner's Sons, 1971), pp. 83–93.

3. Phillips, *Emerging Republican Majority*, p. 37.

4. V. O. Key, Jr., with the assistance of Milton C. Cummings, Jr., *The Responsible Electorate* (New York: Vintage Books, 1968),

5. See Robert Agranoff, ed., *The New Style in Election Campaigns* (Boston: Holbrook Press, 1972) for an interesting collection of articles which deal with the power of the media in political campaigns.

6. Key, *Responsible Electorate*, pp. 7-8.

7. Ibid., p. 60.

8. Ibid., p. 62

9. Ibid., p. 52 ff.

10. An interesting study which considers both party identification and coalitions formed in response to short-term trends is found in Robert Axelrod, "Where the Votes Come From: An Analysis of Electoral Coalitions, 1952–1968," *American Political Science Review*, Vol. 66, No. 1 (March 1972), pp. 11–20.

11. Angus Campbell, Gerald Gurin, and Warren E. Miller, *The Voter Decides* (Evanston, Ill.: Row, Peterson & Co., 1954), pp. 86–87.

12. Ibid., p. 90.

13. Ibid. p. 91.

14. Ibid. p. 92.

15. Angus Campbell, Philip E. Converse, Warren E. Miller, and Donald E. Stokes, *The American Voter* (New York: John Wiley & Sons, 1960), pp. 13–14.

16. Ibid., p. 9.

17. Ibid., p. 29. Also see pp. 24–37 for a comprehensive discussion of the concept of the "funnel of causality."

18. Ibid., p. 33.

19. Ibid., p. 35.

20. Ibid., p. 66.

21. Ibid., p. 122 ff. The seven classifications of voters established were: Strong Republicans, Weak Republicans, Independent Republi-

cans, Independents, Independent Democrats, Weak Democrats, Apolitical, or Don't Know. Voters were placed in these categories according to their answers to the following questions:

Generally speaking, do you think of yourself as a Republican, a Democrat, an Independent, or what?

Those who identified with either party were asked:

Would you call yourself a strong (Republican, Democrat) or a not very strong (Republican, Democrat)?

Those who called themselves Independents were asked:

Do you think of yourself as closer to the Republican or Democratic Party?

22. Ibid., p. 128

23. Ibid., p. 36.

24. Paul F. Lazarsfeld, Bernard Berelson, and Hazel Gaudet, *The People's Choice*, 3rd ed. (New York: Columbia University Press, 1968), p. 10.

25. Ibid., p. 69. It should be noted that this passage refers to voters who switch during the campaign rather than from one Presidential election to the next.

26. Ibid., p. 101.

27. Ibid., pp. 170–71.

28. Campbell, Gurin, and Miller, *Voter Decides*, p. 85.

29. Morris Janowitz and Dwaine Marvick, *Competitive Pressure and Democratic Consent* (Chicago: Quadrangle Books, 1964), p. 92.

30. Bernard R. Berelson, Paul F. Lazarsfeld, and William McPhee, *Voting* (Chicago: University of Chicago Press, 1954), p. 20.

31. Ibid., p. 20.

32. Ibid., p. 27.

33. Ibid., p. 147.

34. Philip E. Converse, "The Concept of a Normal Vote," in Angus Campbell, Philip E. Converse, Warren E. Miller, and Donald E. Stokes, *Elections and the Political Order* (New York: John Wiley & Sons, 1966), p. 18 ff.

35. Data on turnout in Presidential elections will be presented later in this book. In general, those at the lower end of the socioeconomic scale vote less.

36. Angus Campbell, "A Classification of the Presidential Elections," in *Elections and the Political Order*, p. 63. Also see Philip E. Converse, Angus Campbell, Warren E. Miller, Donald E. Stokes, "Stability and Change in 1960: A Reinstating Election," in the same work, pp. 78–95.

This chapter introduces the idea of a "reinstating" election, one in which the majority party is returned to the Presidency.

37. Campbell, "Classification of Presidential Elections," p. 64.

38. Ibid., p. 69.

39. Ibid., p. 74. The realigning election was first postulated by V. O. Key, Jr., as a "critical" election in "A Theory of Critical Elections," *Journal of Politics*, Vol. 17, No. 1 (February 1955), pp. 3–18. Also see Charles G. Sellars, Jr., "The Equilibrium Cycle in Two-Party Politics," *Public Opinion Quarterly*, Vol. 29 (Spring 1965), pp. 15–38.

3 The Party Faithful and the Independents

The theories of voting behavior and classifications of Presidential elections discussed in Chapter 2 are all based on the assumption that party loyalty is a stable and pervasive influence on voting behavior. Different explanations are advanced for this phenomenon, and varying degrees of emphasis are placed upon the impact of partisanship.

That party loyalty is generally stable over time has been indicated by data such as that given in Table 3-1 below. Most Americans obviously do form a psychological or emotional attachment to either the Democratic or Republican Party. Our interest in the extent to which expressions of party identification are reflected by voting behavior also sheds light on the relative size of the bloc of voters who switch parties in Presidential elections regardless of their party identification. These are the Independent voters, if voting behavior is the criterion of independency.[1]

The question of why people vote as they do is as important as the determination of how they vote. Do the Independents exhibit different political characteristics than Democrats or Republicans? Is there a marked difference between Democrats and Republicans? Data in this chapter will explore these questions, and other possible differences in these voting groups will be examined throughout the book. An understanding of the forces which motivate the American electorate is essential to an appreciation of the role Presidential elections play in the political process.

Note: See footnote 21, Chapter 2, for the questions asked of respondents to establish their party self-identification.

THE PARTY FAITHFUL

The most forceful proponents of the importance of party self-identification are the authors of *The Voter Decides* and *The American Voter*,[2] which were discussed in Chapter 2. In the latter the statement is made that "Evidently no single datum can tell us more about the attitude and behavior of the individual as presidential elector than his location on a dimension of psychological identification extending between the two great parties."[3]

Party identification is at the core of psychological theory of voting behavior, which avers that the voting decision is primarily shaped by psychological predispositions. Table 3-1 offers an opportunity to observe trends in party identification, which is seen as the most important variable in psychological theory. The percentage of the electorate identifying as Democrats (strong and weak) dropped from 47 percent in 1952 to 41 percent in 1972. There was a corresponding drop of 4 percent in the number of Republican identifiers. The Independents rose from 22 percent in 1952 to 34 percent in 1972.

Thus, despite the tendency for more voters to describe themselves as Independents, about two-thirds of the electorate still identify with the Democratic or Republican Party. And about two-thirds of the party identifiers are Democrats. How do these data relate to the results of Presidential elections since 1952? The Republicans have won four of the six contests in the period covered in Table 3-1, despite the fact that only about

TABLE 3-1

PARTY SELF-IDENTIFICATION

	1952	1956	1960	1964	1968	1972
Democrat						
Strong	22%	21%	20%	26%	20%	15%
Weak	25	23	25	25	25	26
Independent						
Democrat	10	7	7	9	10	11
Independent	5	9	10	8	11	13
Republican	7	8	7	6	9	10
Republican						
Strong	13	15	14	11	10	10
Weak	14	14	13	13	14	13
Apolitical,						
Don't Know	4	3	4	2	1	2
Totals	100%	100%	100%	100%	100%	100%
Number of cases	1,614	1,772	1,954	1,571	1,553	2,703

Source: Survey Research Center

one-quarter of the electorate identified itself with the Grand Old Party in that period. This is an indication that a sufficient number of American voters are Independent enough in voting behavior to allow the Republican Party success in Presidential elections. The rise in the percentage of professed Independents and the decline in those who claim partisanship is further indication that the importance of party labels in Presidential elections has declined markedly in the past two decades.

Partisans and Presidential Elections

Table 3-2 shows the breakdown of votes for President among Democrats, Republicans, and Independents during the same

TABLE 3-2

PERCENTAGE OF POPULAR VOTE BY GROUPS IN PRESIDENTIAL ELEC-
TIONS, 1952-72

	National	Republicans	Democrats	Independents
1952				
Stevenson	44.6%	9%	77%	35%
Eisenhower	55.4	92	23	65
1956				
Stevenson	42.2	4	85	30
Eisenhower	57.8	96	15	70
1960				
Kennedy	50.1	5	84	43
Nixon	49.9	95	16	57
1964				
Johnson	61.3	20	87	56
Goldwater	38.7	80	13	44
1968				
Humphrey	43.0	9	74	31
Nixon	43.4	86	12	44
Wallace	13.6	5	14	25
1972				
McGovern	38	5	67	31
Nixon	62	95	33	69

Source: Gallup Opinion Index, December 1972, Report No. 90.

period. The Republican Presidential candidates have done well
among the Independents in their successful campaigns. Dwight
Eisenhower garnered about two-thirds of the Independent vote
in his two elections, and Richard Nixon did the same in 1972.
The addition of George Wallace to the slate in 1968 cut into the
Republican share of the Independent vote, but it was substan-
tially greater than the Democrats' share. The only election of
the six included in the table in which the Democrats won a
majority of the Independent vote was 1964. This election provides an interesting insight into the question of whether
self-styled Independents are more likely to support Republican

candidates. Although Lyndon Johnson received 56 percent of the Independent vote in his landslide victory, this was less than Eisenhower and Nixon received from this segment of the electorate, except in 1968. Thus Independents do appear inclined to support Republican candidates.

The differences in the pattern of defection from party among Democrats and Republicans are revealing. In the Johnson landslide victory over Barry Goldwater in 1964, 20 percent of Republican identifiers voted against their party's candidate, whereas the Republican landslide in 1972 was achieved with the help of 33 percent of the Democrats. If we assume that the greatest degree of defection will occur in landslide contests, Republicans appear more steadfast in their party loyalty than Democrats do. The percentage of Democrats leaving their party in the other elections since 1952 is also much greater than that of Republicans. This helps to explain the success of the Republican Party in Presidential elections. The willingness of Democratic identifiers to vote for Republican Presidential candidates offsets the Democratic edge in party identification.

Differences in Party Loyalty

Within the broad categories of Democrats, Republicans, and Independents there are gradations of partisanship and independence. The extent to which expressions of party identification may explain or predict the voting behavior of an individual in Presidential elections is a function of both the intensity of party loyalty and short-term factors which may deflect this loyalty. The three Presidential elections of the 1960s provide an interesting view of the stability of party loyalty in the face of atypical political events which accompanied each election. The impact of John Kennedy's Catholicism in 1960 injected a new element into Presidential campaigns. If religion is an important consideration to the American electorate, substantial party defections should have been expected. The extremism of Goldwater in 1964 was also an unusual factor in Presidential elections since World War II, which have been marked by a lack of ideological fervor. The candidacy of Wallace in 1968 was another unknown in the elections of the 1960s, all three of which were marked by factors which had the potential to upset the normal voting habits of the individual.

Table 3-3 sheds light on the relationship between party identification and reported voting behavior during the 1960s elections. The strong identifiers in both parties did, indeed cast their ballots in a manner consistent with their avowed loyalty. The Strong Republicans were more likely to support their party's candidate than the Strong Democrats were. The percentage of strong identifiers in both parties that remained loyal despite the infusion of unusual short-term factors is impressive both in its size and in its resistance to change over the period of three elections.

Approximately three-quarters of the Strong Democrats and five-sixths of the Strong Republicans form the core of support that their respective parties can build upon in each Presidential election. Table 3-1 shows that the percentage of strong party identifiers, both Democrat and Republican, decreased from 35 percent in 1952 to 25 percent in 1972. As we approach the 1976 Presidential election the groups of voters the Democrats and Republicans can consider safely in their camps are rather small. If we relate the percentage of strong identifiers in Table 3-1 to the reported vote of that group in Table 3-3, we find that about 11 percent of the electorate is very likely to vote for the Democratic Presidential candidate regardless of short-term considerations. The Republicans can count on about 8 percent as their hard-core base of support. These percentages demonstrate that the two major parties have a very small group of party faithful, and the quantitative difference between the parties is not great.[4]

The percentages in Table 3-3 tend to exaggerate the impact of partisanship. The demonstrated loyalty of the strong identifiers over the span of three elections conceals defections within the group from election to election. These do not change the overall percentage of loyalists, but they do increase the number of strong identifiers who are willing to vote against their party.

TABLE 3—3

RELATIONSHIP OF POSTELECTION REPORTED VOTE TO PARTY
SELF-IDENTIFICATION 1960—68

Reported Vote	Party Self-Identification						
	Strong Demo- crat %	Weak Demo- crat %	Inde- pendent Demo- crat %	Inde- pendent %	Inde- pendent Repub- lican %	Weak Repub- lican %	Strong Repub- lican %
1960							
Democratic	73.8	55.3	68.3	35.7	9.6	15.3	0.6
Republican	9.3	24.4	7.9	39.8	74.0	72.0	91.6
Nonvoter,inap.	16.9	21.3	23.8	24.5	16.4	12.7	7.8
	100.0	100.0	100.0	100.0	100.0	100.0	100.0
No. of cases— 1,087							
1964							
Democratic	77.4	59.1	63.3	44.8	21.0	36.5	8.9
Republican	3.8	12.9	7.0	13.3	63.0	47.9	82.8
Nonvoter,inap.	18.8	28.0	29.7	41.9	16.0	15.6	8.3
	100.0	100.0	100.0	100.0	100.0	100.0	100.0
No. of cases— 1,438							
1968							
Democratic	67.0	38.8	35.6	15.0	3.2	7.8	2.2
Republican	6.2	18.8	20.7	34.3	65.1	65.1	81.3
Wallace	6.2	10.4	11.9	12.9	11.1	11.1	1.4
Nonvoter,inap.	20.6	32.0	31.8	37.8	20.6	16.0	15.1
	100.0	100.0	100.0	100.0	100.0	100.0	100.0
No. of cases— 1,385							

Source: Survey Research Center.   *inap.-inappropriate

THE INDEPENDENTS

The nature of the Independent voter has long been a source of interest. The idea that he differs in terms of political interest or knowledge from voters who identify themselves as partisans has been widely stated by students of voting behavior.[5] The consensus is that political interest level is highly related to political partisanship—the more partisan, the more interest in Presidential elections.

The first prominent statements of this idea were set forth in *The People's Choice* and *Voting*.[6] While these studies were primarily concerned with intracampaign behavior, the link between partisanship and level of interest has been accepted by most observers. In *The People's Choice* it is stated that most voters who changed their vote intention during the campaign were disinterested, poorly informed, and apathetic toward the election.[7] In *Voting*, stability in vote is called characteristic of those interested in politics, while instability characterizes those not particularly interested.[8] These authors go on to say that "partisanship increases political interest," and "anything that weakens partisan feelings decreases interest,"[9] a dictum applied to those who change vote intention between campaigns as well as during campaigns.[10] This line of thought is also accepted in *The American Voter*, and Angus Campbell further endorses the idea that those most interested in politics are the strongest party identifiers.[11]

The Politically Aware Independent

Table 3-4 relates political interest to party identification. Strong identifiers—both Democratic and Republican—express more political interest than weak identifiers do, while Independents leaning to either party demonstrate more political interest than those who classify themselves solely as Independents. Table 3-4 highlights the Independent "leaners" to either party as the most politically interested segment of the

TABLE 3-4

RELATIONSHIP OF POLITICAL INTEREST TO PARTY SELF-IDENTIFICATION, 1968

Reported Degree to which Politics Is Followed	Party Self-Identification						
	Strong Demo-crat %	Weak Demo-crat %	Inde-pendent Demo-crat %	Inde-pendent %	Inde-pendent Repub-lican %	Weak Repub-lican %	Strong Repub-lican %
Very closely	36.9	30.7	44.1	25.5	57.5	39.0	49.7
Fairly closely	31.7	29.5	33.6	35.4	29.1	35.0	30.6
Not much	31.4	39.8	22.3	39.1	13.4	26.0	19.7
	100.0	100.0	100.0	100.0	100.0	100.0	100.0
No. of cases	309	387	152	161	134	226	147

Source: Survey Research Center.

electorate. It is also interesting to note that Strong Republicans have levels of interest closer to those of the Independent "leaners" than to those of the Strong Democrats. This indicates that party allegiance is not as related to political interest in the case of Democrats as it is in the Republican instance.

Obviously, assertions that political interest and strong party identification are closely related are not supported by the data in Table 3-4. Strong Democrats show considerably less interest than either Republicans or all Independents as a group. The differences observed between those who identify as Independent as opposed to those who identify as Independents leaning to a party are noteworthy. The former are the least interested voters, while the latter are among those of highest interest. This suggests that when asked about party identification very few voters with any interest will declare no partiality to either party. Political parties are an ingrained part of the American political culture, and it is to be expected that most respondents will identify with either the Democrats or the Republicans at some level of politics.

Independents have been found to express less concern about the outcome of Presidential elections than partisans.[12] However, this is not a contradiction of Table 3-4, which demonstrates that Independents have as much or more political interest than strong party identifiers. The explanation lies in the fact that political interest and concern about the outcome of a Presidential election are not analogous, although they are often treated as one. Robert E. Agger notes that "The political interests of the Independent go only so far; they stop short of viewing the other (party) as a very significant threat to the country."[13] The Independent voter can thus combine interest and knowledge with a low level of concern. The data presented earlier in this chapter indicate that this is also true of the substantial numbers of voters who, regardless of party loyalty, vote for the Presidential candidate of the other party if sufficiently motivated.

It is somewhat incongruous that most voting behaviorists have viewed independence in voting as a characteristic of the politically inferior. If one is to be loyal, there must be an organizational structure or ideological framework to command loyalty. It would be difficult indeed to describe either of our national parties in terms that suggest a permanent, stable organization with which voters are likely to identify.

Not all scholars have viewed the Independent voter as an aberration in our political system. Murray S. Stedman, Jr., and Herbert Sonthoff expressed it this way:

> If . . . the term [Independent] refers to the shifting of voters from one party to the other in general elections, it is difficult to see the basis for the objection to this practice. A voter who changes parties in elections can hardly be termed "independent" in the sense he repudiates parties. To the contrary, such a voter is presumably responsible for forcing the parties to commit themselves to programs at all![14]

The view that those who switch parties in Presidential elections have different political characteristics than avowed partisans is also rejected by V. O. Key, Jr.:

... the switchers, who (in company with 'new' voters) call the turn, are persons whose peculiarity is not lack of interest but agreement on broad political issues with the standpatters toward whom they shift. ... This should be regarded as at least a modicum of evidence for the view that those who switch do so to support governmental policies or outlooks with which they agree, not because of subtle psychological or sociological peculiarities.[15]

This view of voting behavior places primary emphasis on short-term political factors rather than on the impact of party identification. Key endorses the latter force to a limited extent, noting that "those who agree with their party are most inclined to stay with it."[16] But he believes that voter perceptions of the performance of the party in power are the most important influence on the voting decision.

Party Loyalty and the Political Climate

The relative importance of short-term political considerations and party loyalty is impossible to quantify. The materials reviewed in this chapter suggest that the percentage of voters who are willing to vote for the Presidential candidates of either party is much greater than the number who identify as Independents (Table 3-1). Only the bulk of strong identifiers within the Democratic and Republican Parties is likely to remain steadfast, regardless of short-term political events. Many of those in the weak and independent categories of party identifiers can be deflected from their usual voting pattern by contemporary events.

Survey Research Center data for 1972 indicate that when 2,073 people were asked: "Have you always voted for the same party or have you voted for different parties for President?" 46 percent replied they voted for the same party, while 54 percent indicated they voted for different parties. Thus over half of the electorate reported having voted for Presidential candidates of more than one party. The potential percentage of voting Independents is much greater than those who have switched parties in the past. The data include those who have only voted once or twice, and these voters are potential Independents, although to date they have voted for the candidate of a single party.[17]

Despite the indicated large Democratic margin in party loyalty, both parties attract similar minimum support when they lose. In the Johnson landslide of 1964, the Republican Party attracted about 38 percent of the vote. The Democratic Party garnered about the same percentage in the wake of Nixon's 1972 sweep. Protestations of partisanship or independence notwithstanding, this appears to be about the minimal percentage of the vote either of the major parties is likely to attract in a two-party race. The reversal of party landslides in 1964 and 1972 gives further evidence that the American voter views Presidential elections as an opportunity to pass judgment on incumbent administrations and candidates. The influence of partisanship on such judgments is far weaker than has been assumed.

If Presidential elections are, as we believe, interpreted by the electorate as expressions of approval or disapproval of incumbent administrations, it is not surprising that the losing party maintains support from more than a third of the voters. There is a dualism in national politics that is due to the finite nature of national resources. Any legislation or program aids one segment of the population at the expense of others. The successful President avoids infuriating the many for the benefit of the few. The Democratic reign in the White House during the Roosevelt and Truman administrations is offered by many as evidence of a period of one-party dominance. The question is whether the Democrats retained power because of party loyalty or because the majority of the electorate approved of their administrations. One prominent observer wrote: "... The misfortunes of the Republicans over the period 1932–52 sprang essentially from the simple fact that they could not lay their hands on an issue on which the Democrats had outraged enough people to vote them out of office."[18] It should be noted that during this era of Democratic dominance the Republicans never received less than 36.5 percent of the vote (Landon's share in the 1936 election). American political parties are noted for their lack of ideological appeal to the electorate.[19] It would be surprising, indeed, if the pragmatic approach of either party were capable of producing any large number of party zealots.

NOTES

1. An alternate definition of the Independent voter is offered in Walter DeVries and V. Lance Tarrance, *The Ticket-Splitter* (Grand Rapids, Mich.: William B. Eerdmans Publishing Co., 1972), p. 23: "True independence is defined in this book as actual ticket-splitting, since this is what ultimately counts at the campaign level."

2. Angus Campbell; Gerald Gurin, and Warren E. Miller, *The Voter Decides* (Evanston, Ill.: Row, Peterson & Co., 1954), and Angus Campbell, Philip E. Converse, Warren E. Miller, and Donald Stokes, *The American Voter* (New York: John Wiley & Sons, 1960).

3. Campbell, Converse, and Miller, *American Voter,* pp. 142–43.

4. Gerald Pomper, *Elections in America* (New York: Dodd, Mead & Co., 1970), pp. 92–98.

5. See Samuel J. Eldersveld, "The Independent Vote: Measurement, Characteristics, and Implications for Party Strategy," *American Political Science Review,* Vol. 46. No. 3 (September 1952), pp. 732–53; Philip K. Hastings, "The Independent Voter in 1952: A Study of Pittsfield, Massachusetts," *American Political Science Review,* No. 47, September 1953, pp. 805–10; Robert E. Agger, "Independents and Party Identifiers: Characteristics and Behavior in 1952," in Eugene Burdick and Arthur J. Brodbeck, eds., *American Voting Behavior* (Glencoe, Ill.: Free Press, 1959), pp. 308–29.

6. Paul Lazarsfeld, Bernard Berelson, and Hazel Gaudet, *The People's Choice* (New York: Columbia University Press, 1944), and Bernard R. Berelson, Paul F. Lazarsfeld, and William N. McPhee, *Voting* (Chicago: University of Chicago Press, 1954).

7. Lazarsfeld, Berelson, and Gaudet, *The People's Choice,* p. 69.

8. Berelson, Lazarsfeld, and McPhee, *Voting,* p. 20.

9. Ibid., p. 27.

10. Ibid., p. 33.

11. Angus Campbell, "Voters and Elections: Past and Present," *Journal of Politics,* 26, 1964, p. 356.

12. William H. Flanigan, *Political Behavior of the American Electorate* (Boston: Allyn and Bacon, 1968), pp. 43–44.

13. Robert E. Agger, "Independents and Party Identifiers: Characteristics and Behavior in 1952," in Burdick and Brodbeck, eds., *American Voting Behavior*, p. 327.

14. Murray S. Stedman, Jr., and Herbert Sonthoff, "Party Responsibility – A Critical Inquiry," in John R. Owens and P. J. Staudenraus, eds., *The American Party System* (New York: Macmillan Co., 1965), p. 451.

15. V. O. Key, Jr., with the assistance of Milton C. Cummings, Jr., *The Responsible Electorate* (New York: Vintage Books, 1968), p. 104.

16. Ibid., p. 150.

17. An excellent study which deals largely with the interpretation of voting studies is H. Daubt, *Floating Voters and the Floating Vote* (Leiden: H. E. Stenfert-Kroese N.V., 1961).

18. Key, *Responsible Electorate*, p. 62.

19. Herbert McClosky, Paul J. Hoffman, and Rosemary O'Hara, "Issue Conflict and Consensus among Party Leaders and Followers," *American Political Science Review*, Vol. 54, No. 2. June 1960, pp. 425–26.

4 Group Voting Behavior in Presidential Elections

Voters casting their ballots for the Republican or Democratic Party share a similarity in social and economic orientation and characteristics with many of their fellow supporters of a particular candidate. Concepts of group voting behavior are related to (1) learning whether different sociological types are attracted to the respective major parties, (2) attempting to identify the various groups that form electoral coalitions within the major parties, and (3) determining the relative permanence or transience of these coalitions. Political analysts assess the election prospects of Presidential candidates by reference to geographic, racial, ethnic, occupational, religious, educational, and age groupings within the voting public. They attempt to ascertain the political leanings of these various groups and use that information to reach their judgments of the candidate's prospects.

The People's Choice was one of the first voting studies to stress the relationship between sociological factors and voting behavior.[1] The statements that "a person thinks, politically, as he is, socially" and that "Social characteristics determine political preference"[2] imply that American political parties are class based. Holding that "Any practical politician worth his salt knows a great deal about the stratification of the American electorate," this study maintains that no politician would "be in business long if he did not know who was most susceptible to the arguments of either party."[3]

The voting choice of an individual is based on perceptions of his own interest as well as national interests.[4] We will explore the extent to which these perceptions are affected by sociological characteristics or group identity.

THE INCREASINGLY AFFLUENT AND INDEPENDENT ELECTORATE

There is broad agreement that familial influence is a major force in shaping political attitudes. This is attributed to the depth of psychological influences created by the proximal relationship of the family group. In terms of voting behavior, however, the real question is the impact of the primary group influence over time. Given the upward social mobility of large segments of American society, it seems reasonable to assume that parental influence will weaken with the passage of time. As new voters are exposed to new sources of politicization—such as peer groups in college—attitudes are formed that may differ markedly from those of the family. Pollster Louis Harris's data led him to this conclusion:

> The essential truth was that, once a person was sprung loose from the traditional world of family background, ethnic environment, geographical neighborhoods, and exposed to the broader horizons of a college education, no matter how full of shortfalls, there was little likelihood of the college product returning to the mold from whence he came.[5]

The degree of influence of primary relationships in adulthood is more a function of similarity of socioeconomic status than a psychological carry-over. The impact of continually higher levels of education and income on the American political system can hardly be exaggerated. Increasingly, voters will be influenced less by their early politicization, which often includes traditions of family loyalty to a political party.

Table 4-1 shows the relationship between education and income. The recent dramatic rise in the educational level of American voters has important political implications. Political awareness and knowledge are within the grasp of an increasing percentage of the electorate. As an individual's feeling of political efficacy increases, there is likely to be less reliance on traditional reference points such as parties.

TABLE 4—1

RELATIONSHIP BETWEEN INCOME AND EDUCATION
(Percentage of individuals with varying levels of education, who reach various maximum incomes)

| | Education Level Achieved | | |
Maximum Annual Income	8th Grade or Less	High School	Some College
Under $5,000	59%	17%	11%
$5,000–9,999	29	41	26
$10,000–14,999	9	30	24
$15,000 and over	3	12	39

Source: The Harris Survey, March 1973

The higher educational level of Americans is accompanied by steady increases in income. Table 4-2 demonstrates the increasing affluence of the U.S. citizen. The steady increase in income which has occurred and is projected reduces the impact of economic class as a determinant of voting behavior. American political parties must direct their appeals to an increasingly affluent citizenry and one which has less fear of such personal economic perils as unemployment. Indeed, a society in which 6 percent unemployment is considered unacceptable as a matter of public policy offers little hope for partisan appeals based upon economic strata.

TABLE 4—2

INCOME CHANGES IN U.S. FROM 1956 PROJECTED TO 1980
(Percentage of families with various levels of annual income)*

Annual Income	1956	1968	1980 (est.)
Under $10,000	82%	60%	39%
$10,000– 14,999	13	25	27
$15,000 and over	5	15	34

*Based on 1968 constant dollars, assuming average inflationary growth of 3.5% per year.

Source: Louis Harris, *The Anguish of Change* (New York: W. W. Norton & Co., 1973), p. 39. Data extracted from *Conference Board Report*, 1968.

As the nation becomes increasingly middle class, the economic issues that will be salient will revolve around problems that cut across income groupings. The energy crisis that emerged in late 1973 is an example of such an issue. It affected all levels of the economic system, and political controversy regarding it centered upon management of the situation rather than harm to a particular income stratum. This is strikingly different from the situation in the 1930s, when depression and widespread unemployment led individuals to look to the political parties for solutions to their economic woes.

The impact of higher educational and income levels can best be illustrated by noting some key characteristics of younger voters. Table 4–3 classifies voters under 30 by education, color, and political identification.

The percentages of eligible voters under 30 identifying themselves as Democratic, Republican, or Independent are much closer than they are for the entire electorate, as shown in Table 3–1 in the preceding chapter. The large group of Independents and the more balanced strength of the two major parties may foretell a political era of increased emphasis on issues and less party influence in Presidential elections.

The nonwhite registration offers evidence that the younger segment of potential black voters is as politically involved as the

TABLE 4—3

REGISTERED VOTERS UNDER 30 YEARS OLD, 1972 PRESIDENTIAL ELECTION
(Percentage of eligible voters registered)

	Percent Registered
All voters under 30	54%
College	67
Noncollege	47
Whites	54
Nonwhites	57
Republicans	58
Democrats	60
Independents	49

Note: Percentages are the total of percentages reported among (1) all eligible voters under 30, (2) new voters 18–24 years old, and (3) the 25–29-year-old group. They thus total over 100 percent.

Source: The Gallup opinion index, August 1972, Report No. 86.

whites in this age group. The traditionally low levels of black registration belong to an older generation, and the black population can now be expected to vote in percentages approximating the rest of the nation. If the pattern of black support of Democratic Presidential candidates continues, this will be an increasingly strong source of support for them. But the percentages of party identifiers and Independents indicate that the black vote may become more fragmented as more of them participate in the political process. The disparity between those with some college who have registered as opposed to the balance of the potential voters under 30 is an indication of both rising educational levels and the strong relationship between education and political participation. It is important, moreover, to differentiate between registration and actual voting turnout, which will be discussed later in the book.

The picture of the electorate presented thus far in this chapter suggests an increasingly affluent, well-educated body of voters with decreasing allegiance to the political ties of their parents. It would be surprising, indeed, if traditional family party loyalties would in any way prevent the younger, well-educated voter from finding his own political direction.

GROUP VOTING BEHAVIOR

There are many other groups in our society that are important politically and give evidence of a certain degree of political homogeneity. The idea of shared attitudes is vital to group identification if it is to have electoral relevance. Members of the Rotary International, for instance, would not be expected to have shared political attitudes, because the organization is apolitical. On the other hand, a high degree of political cohesiveness in the Americans for Democratic Action is to be expected because of its political orientation. Many groups are politically active only in spheres which affect their special interest; an example is the American Medical Association. The degree to which any organization influences the vote of its members is difficult to measure. It is reasonable to assume that the most overtly political organizations will exert the most influence of this type. In this instance, however, the effect is more of a reinforcing element, because the members joined the group in recognition of its political bias.

Both the Democratic and Republican parties have traditionally had the support of specific groups over a period of time. Some of these are political interest groups; the National Association of Manufacturers supports the Republicans and most labor unions have supported Democratic candidates. Other groups with traditional ties are racial or ethnic; both the Jewish and the black votes have been overwhelmingly Democratic since the Roosevelt years. Presidential candidates of either party will take campaign positions calculated to ensure the continued support of these groups.

Both parties have also had the support of specific geographic areas over extended periods. The solidarity of the Democratic

South, for example, was a fact of political life until the 1950s. Likewise, the Republican Party has been able to count upon the support of those in the farm belt and rural areas. These geographical groupings may produce corresponding social groups that tend to support one party, or the other. The rural areas are largely Protestant, and it could be accurately stated that most Protestants have usually supported Republican presidential candidates.

Table 4-4, which illustrates Presidential voting by major groups in the population since 1952, affords an opportunity to distinguish change or similarity in the loyalties of key segments of American society. The group which has remained most steadfast in its voting behavior is the nonwhites (most of whom are blacks). This is the only group in Table 4-4 that has supported one party (in this case the Democrats) in every election from 1952 to 1972. It is interesting to note that the percentage of nonwhites voting Democratic has increased markedly in the past three elections.

The 1972 election found a majority of Catholic voters supporting the Republican candidate for the first time in this two-decade period. This election also saw a shift in another normally Democratic bloc—manual workers. About half had voted for Dwight Eisenhower in 1956, but well over half voted for Richard Nixon in 1972. This group of voters, which accounts for more than a third of the electorate, has been the mainstay of Democratic Presidential candidates since Roosevelt.

The Presidential voting behavior of the groups in Table 4-4 indicates that the Democrats, Republicans, and Independents are heterogeneous groups.[6] None of the groups (with the exception of the nonwhite) consistently voted overwhelmingly for the candidates of either party. This is both a cause and an effect of broad-based appeals by the two major parties, and a resultant lack of ideological fervor that could be translated according to class. How do we reconcile this conclusion with the oft-stated description of the Democratic Party as the "working-man's party" and the Republican Party as the party of "privilege"?

TABLE 4 – 4A

VOTE BY GROUPS IN PRESIDENTIAL ELECTIONS, 1952-60

| | 1952 | | 1956 | | 1960 | |
	Steven-son	Ike	Steven-son	Ike	JFK	Nixon
National	44.6	55.4	42.2	57.8	50.1	49.9
Men	47	53	45	55	52	48
Women	42	58	39	61	49	51
White	43	57	41	59	49	51
Nonwhite	79	21	61	39	68	32
College	34	66	31	69	39	61
High School	45	55	42	58	52	48
Grade School	52	48	50	50	55	45
Professions & Business	36	64	32	68	42	58
White Collar	40	60	37	63	48	52
Manual	55	45	50	50	60	40
Under 30 years	51	49	43	57	54	46
32–49 years	47	53	45	55	54	46
50 years & older	39	61	39	61	46	54
Protestants	37	63	37	63	38	62
Catholics	56	44	51	49	78	22
Republicans	8	92	4	96	5	95
Democrats	77	23	85	15	84	16
Independents	35	65	30	70	43	57
Members of labor union families	61	39	57	43	65	35

Source: The Gallup Opinion Index, December 1972, Report No. 90.

Sociological classification of the electorate according to income, occupation, religion, and education was generally believed to be a valid guide to political behavior until about 1948. The steadily rising percentage of families with incomes over $10,000 (Table 4-2) has increased the number of voters whose economic ties to

TABLE 4 — 4B

VOTE BY GROUPS IN PRESIDENTIAL ELECTIONS, 1964–72

	1964			1968		1972	
	LBJ	Gold-water	HHH	Nixon	Wallace	McGov-ern	Nixon
National	61.3	38.7	43.0	43.4	13.6	38	62
Men	60	40	41	43	16	37	63
Women	62	38	45	43	12	38	62
White	59	41	38	47	15	32	68
Nonwhite	94	6	85	12	3	87	13
College	52	48	37	54	9	37	63
High School	62	38	42	43	15	34	66
Grade School	66	34	52	33	15	49	51
Professions & Business	54	46	34	56	10	31	69
White Collar	57	43	41	47	12	36	64
Manual	71	29	50	35	15	43	57
Under 30 years	64	36	47	38	15	48	52
32–49 years	63	37	44	41	15	33	67
50 years & older	59	41	41	47	12	36	64
Protestants	55	45	35	49	16	30	70
Catholics	76	24	59	33	8	48	52
Republicans	20	80	9	86	5	5	95
Democrats	87	13	74	12	14	67	33
Independents	56	44	31	44	25	31	69
Members of labor union families	73	27	56	29	15	46	54

Source: The Gallup Opinion Index, December 1972, Report No. 90.

the Democratic Party have weakened or disappeared. This does not indicate that they have turned to the Republican Party en masse, but it does help explain the increased independence of the American voter as party ties wither. The increase in educational levels also has helped mute the differences in the basis of support for the parties.[7]

Those theorists who emphasized the importance of sociological factors in voting behavior were writing in the pre-1948 period. The change from the depression psychology of the 1930s to the postwar affluence from about 1948 on brought about a change in the electorate's perceptions of political reality. It has been observed that "Socio-economic status continues to operate in politics but not with the monolithic force that Marx attributed to it and by no means with sole reference to economic status."[8] The fact that the distribution of income and education cuts across party lines is important to the stability of the country's party system. The tendency to use class-based appeals is largely muted by the desire to attract support from all quarters.[9]

CROSS-PRESSURES

One of the major difficulties in determining group influence on voting behavior is that most people have an affinity for more than one group. A voter may belong both to a labor union, which usually supports Democratic candidates, and to the American Legion, which is more apt to have a Republican outlook. Many individuals also feel a bond with racial, religious, or ethnic groups which have a degree of political homogeneity.

These various emotional ties can result in cross-pressures upon the individual in terms of political orientation. For group membership to be significant in political terms, however, it is essential that the voter translate his affinity with a particular group in a political manner. A union member whose membership is predicated solely on the requirement that he join to fulfill employment requirements is less likely to take his political clues from the union leadership than is the committed unionist who looks to the organization for interpretations of political events. Nor should we assume that the same influence will always be predominant in the political views of all members of the group. Indeed, "There are dangers in attributing to any individual the behavioral characteristics of the group he belongs to.... He is ... differentiated from others in the group by personality, attitudes, motivations, and habits of mind that diverge in subtle and complex ways from a modal pattern."[10]

The presence of cross-pressures and the frailty of generalizations about group voting behavior should be kept in mind in the consideration of coalitions of groups within the Democratic and Republican parties that follows.

COALITIONS

In order to explain voting behavior in Presidential elections by group behavior, it is necessary to introduce the concept of coalition. The generally accepted premise since the 1930s has been that "the Democrats are a coalition of diverse overlapping minorities: the poor, Blacks, union members, Catholics and Jews," whereas "the Republicans can be thought of as a coalition of the nonpoor Whites, nonunion families, Protestants, Northerners, and those outside the central cities."[11] While the groups comprising the Republican coalition are larger in size and have a higher turnout than those in the Democratic coalition, the latter have voted for their party in larger percentages.

The alternation of party power in Presidential elections in the 1952–72 period is evidence that there is considerable shifting both in group support and the percentages of a particular group supporting the party with which they are identified. In a study of electoral coalitions in the 1952–68 period, Robert Axelrod concludes:

> The most obvious fact about American party coalitions is that they are very loose. They are loose first in the sense that most group loyalties are not total. Except for the Blacks, none of the ... groups that have been examined ... ever gave more than 80 per cent of their votes to one party. Second, the coalitions are loose in the sense that group loyalties are not constant from one election to the next. Finally, when a group's loyalty shifts it is as likely to shift in response to a national trend as it is for reasons specific to the group.[12]

Coalitions are subject to the same political stresses as the individual groups of which they are comprised. Politics is a dynamic force in which new issues replace old ones and groups find a community of interest with former antagonists. The swiftly changing face of American society and the efforts of the major parties to benefit from this change provide the cutting edge of modern Presidential electoral competition. Contests for the Presidency offer an overview of geographic, ethnic, religious, racial, and other differences that manifest themselves in political conflict.

ANTIESTABLISHMENT COALITIONS

As societal values change, the emergence of new dimensions of political competition can be observed. The economic conflict that marked national politics before World War II was largely ameliorated by postwar prosperity which has continued to afford jobs and access to the amenities of modern society to most citizens. In the United States of the 1960s and 1970s, one observer notes, "the majority are beyond subsistence concerns, and thus can 'afford' to devote attention to matters of prestige or standing in society."[13]

These status concerns explain much contemporary friction between blacks and whites. The former have raised their economic sights and are now competing for education and housing in urban areas. The busing controversies are an outgrowth of segregated housing and school patterns caused partially by past income disparities. The whites most directly affected by this problem are those in urban areas whose socioeconomic status is usually higher than that of the urban blacks and who feel threatened by the black demand for upward social mobility. The political results of this clash are observable in the swing to the Republican Party in 1972 of blue-collar workers, who had been a mainstay of the Democratic Party (Table 4-4).

The 1972 election thus found the blue-collar worker voting in concert with the bank president, although for different reasons. The latter was not threatened by status conflict within the lower socioeconomic strata and was simply maintaining long-standing political inclinations. Status conflict, then, is unlikely to involve those whose education, skills, and background assure them status. The conflict is contained within the segments of society that feel threatened or are attempting to move up.

McGovern's campaign strategy in 1972 was directed at forming a coalition of the dissatisfied groups: blacks, the poor, college students, and other minorities. One problem was that those groups on the fringe or outside of the establishment had difficulty finding common ground with other antiestablishment groups. As Everett Ladd notes, "What holds one segment together assures that the rest cannot enter a coalition with it."[14]

Those in the mainstream of the establishment are usually able to mute much of the antiestablishment fervor by offering limited opportunity for status advance to particularly militant groups. Efforts by large industrial and banking corporations to improve urban housing, education, and job opportunity offer the inner-city black hope of a better tomorrow. Such programs also mute attempts to build antiestablishment coalitions.

THE ETHNICS

Perhaps the most widely recognized of the electoral coalitions within the two major parties are the ethnic groups. These so-called hyphenated Americans (all those from other than English heritage) are estimated to number about 65 million,[15] a size which explains the attention given the ethnic vote. Members of ethnic groups are, of course, also identified with other groups. The impact of ethnicity on voting behavior is largely a function of individual affinity (or lack of affinity) to the group. The voting behavior of some key ethnic groups in Presidential elections can shed light on their importance in party coalitions.

The black vote was overwhelmingly Republican until the 1934 Congressional elections. This loyalty is explained by the same factor (but with opposite results) as is the Democratic

Solid South—the Civil War. The shift to the Democratic Party by most black voters was caused by the New Deal, which this segment of the population, hard hit by the depression, viewed as helpful. Democratic Presidents since Roosevelt have sponsored legislation to further black progress, and the strongest black support of a Republican candidate since 1936 was the 39 percent who voted for Eisenhower in 1956. The fact that there are approximately 25 million blacks in the United States makes apparent the political potential of this ethnic group. Among all those living in central cities, 23 percent are black, which accentuates the impact of this group on the nation's most populous states. Further, the percentage of blacks voting has increased dramatically. In 1968, 57.6 percent of voting-age blacks cast ballots for President, as compared to 69.1 percent of the eligible white voters.[16] Table 4-4 indicates that this group is very much a part of the contemporary Democratic coalition.

Jewish support for Democratic Presidential candidates is almost as strong: 82 percent of Jewish voters voted Democratic in 1960, 90 percent in 1964, and 83 percent in 1968. The strong Jewish backing of liberal candidates and positions has kept this ethnic group in the Democratic coalition, despite levels of affluence which are usually associated with political conservatism.

The Irish are the most thoroughly assimilated ethnic group. They arrived in this country before the other ethnics (with the exception of the blacks) and comprise one of the largest ethnic blocs—about 13 million. While the past decade has seen lower Irish majorities for Democratic candidates, this group is still part of the Democratic coalition. John Kennedy received 75 percent of the Irish vote in 1960, and Lyndon Johnson did even better in 1964, with 78 percent. Hubert Humphrey received 64 percent of the Irish vote in 1968. There are cross-currents that may alter the tendency of Catholics to support the Democratic Presidential candidate in the future. Among the traditionally conservative Irish there is some indication that there is a shift toward the Republican Party.[17] Whether this will be of sufficient magnitude to represent an Irish bloc is far from certain. It is very possible that this ethnic group will prove relatively independent in voting behavior.

Two other ethnic groups that have consistently voted Democratic in overwhelming proportions are the Slavs and the Italians. Among the Italians, 75 percent voted for Kennedy in 1960, 77 percent for Johnson in 1964, and 60 percent for Humphrey in 1968. The Slavs have given even larger pluralities to Democratic candidates: 82 percent voted for Kennedy, 80 percent for Johnson, and 65 percent for Humphrey. Both groups are heavily blue collar, and 1972 results may well present a picture of a trend toward the Republican Party. But one must be extremely cautious about such generalizations. Any landslide victory, such as Nixon's in 1972, will reflect substantial changes in the partisan mix. This in itself offers no proof that Italian or Slavic voters are turning to the Republican Party. It does indicate that large numbers of these two groups are reasonably independent in their voting decisions in Presidential elections.

References to ethnic groups in discussions of electoral coalitions are based on surveys of voting precincts known to include large majorities of a given ethnic group. This tells us nothing of the voting behavior of Slavs, Italians, and so on who live in areas with few persons of their ethnic background. All of the groups classed as ethnic live predominantly in urban areas. This raises a fundamental question: Is it ethnicity or urban residence that is the most plausible explanation for the support of Democratic Presidential candidates by ethnic blocs? During the era of Republican dominance in Presidential elections that followed the Civil War, the Democrats concentrated their efforts among the newly arrived immigrants, who tended to settle in the larger cities. The party served as an umbrella under which ethnics of all kinds could find a political refuge and which advocated programs designed to help the lower classes find their way into the mainstream of American life.[18] But we have seen evidence of the demise of class as a political arbiter. When we refer to ethnic blocs today it is possibly more a function of geography than origin.

REGIONALISM

Kevin Phillips's *The Emerging Republican Majority* is a
study of voting trends in Presidential elections based largely on
cycles emanating from ideology, population movement, and
regionalism.[19] Phillips views the 1968 election as one in which
realignment of party loyalty was the dominant feature, and Wallace's vote is seen as composed of Democrats on their way to
the Republican Party. This leads to Phillips's observation that
57 percent of the electorate voted against the Democratic candidate. (The actual breakdown was George Wallace, 13.6 percent;
Humphrey 42.7 percent; and Nixon, 43.4 percent.) Phillips argues that the 1968 election marked the movement of heretofore
conservative Democrats—about 15 million in number—to the
Republican Party, with some using the candidacy of Wallace as
a halfway house. The reasons given by Phillips are interesting
though controversial. He alludes to the Democratic Party as the
haven for the "privileged elite, blind to the needs and interests
of the large national majority." He refers to the "vested interests" of this elite in "a high and not necessarily too produc-
tive rate of government social, educational, scientific and research spending."[20] In addition to the ideological backlash he
envisions from the new middle class against these programs,
Phillips views the impact of increased black political participation as the catalyst driving conservative Americans toward the
Republican Party. These trends are expressed geographically by
Phillips: "The upcoming cycle of American politics is likely to
match a dominant Republican Party based in the Heartland,
South and California against a minority Democratic Party based
in the Northeast and Pacific Northwest (and encompassing
Southern as well as Northern Negroes)."[21]

The 1972 election appears to add weight to Phillips's thesis,
unless one chooses to consider George McGovern an atypical
Democratic candidate who adopted positions which were ana-
thema to many potential Democrats. It should also be pointed
out that Presidential incumbents invariably win contests for

reelection. The 1976 Presidential election will prove a test of Phillips's theory. If, in the face of Watergate, the Republican candidate forges a majority from the areas Phillips has circumscribed, we must conclude that a new political cycle did indeed commence in the 1968 election.

Rising levels of income, education, and social status have contributed materially to the diminution of political stratification in American society. Neither party has a monopoly on the votes of any particular group. The tendency of some ethnics — such as Jews, Italians, and Slavs — to overwhelmingly support the Presidential candidate of the Democratic Party may be more a reflection of their immigrant background than an indication of their future behavior as assimilated American voters. The election of Kennedy in 1960 and the absorption of Catholics into the mainstream have largely resolved Protestant-Catholic political separation.

The major dichotomy in American society that still exists, and indeed has intensified in the past decade, is the chasm between black and white America. The gap has widened in political terms because of dramatically increased black participation in the political electoral process. It is doubtful that this will lead to the political realignment Kevin Phillips foresees. The pragmatic, nonideological appeal of American parties is not calculated to encourage the estrangement of any sizable segment of the population from either party. Neither the Democrats, abashed by a resounding defeat in 1972, nor the Republicans, up to their necks in Watergate, are likely to eschew the support of anybody.

NOTES

1. Paul F. Lazarsfeld, Bernard Berelson, and Hazel Gaudet, *The People's Choice* (New York: Columbia University Press, 1944). See Chapter 3 for detailed discussion: "The Social Differences Between Republicans and Democrats."

2. Ibid., p. 27.

3. Ibid., p. 16.

4. James Q. Wilson and Edward C. Banfield, "Public-Regardingness as a Value Premise in Voting Behavior," *The American Political Science Review*, Vol. 58 (December 1964), pp. 876-87. ". . . a considerable proportion of voters, especially in the upper income groups, vote against their self-interest narrowly conceived and . . . a marked ethnic influence appears in the vote," p. 885.

5. Louis Harris, *The Anguish of Change* (New York: W. W. Norton & Co., 1973), p. 43.

6. See William H. Flanigan, *Political Behavior of the American Electorate* (Boston: Allyn & Bacon, 1968), pp. 47-53.

7. Warren E. Miller, "The Political Behavior of the Electorate," in Edward C. Dryer and Walter A. Rosenbaum, eds., *Political Opinion and Electoral Behavior* (Belmont, Cal.: Wadsworth Publishing Co., 1966), pp. 86-97.

8. James C. Davies, *Human Nature in Politics* (New York: John Wiley & Sons, 1963), p. 272.

9. Heinz Eulau, *Class and Party in the Eisenhower Years* (New York: Free Press of Glencoe, 1962), p. 141.

10. Herbert McClosky, "Survey Research in Political Science," in Charles Y. Glock, ed., *Survey Research in the Social Sciences* (New York: Russell Sage Foundation, 1967), pp. 96-97. The study of cross-pressures has failed to yield a theory that satisfactorily explains or predicts their impact on voting behavior. This problem is discussed in (Herbert McClosky and Harold E. Dahlgren) "Primary Group Influence on Party Loyalty," *American Political Science Review*, Vol. 53, No. 3 (September 1959), pp. 763-64, Lazarsfeld, Berelson, and Gaudet, *The People's Choice;* Bernard Berelson, Paul F. Lazarsfeld, and William McPhee, *Voting* (Chicago: University of Chicago Press, 1954); Angus Campbell, Gerald Gurin, and Warren E. Miller, *The Voter Decides* (Evanston, Ill.: Row, Peterson & Co., 1954); Angus Campbell, Philip E. Converse, Warren E. Miller, and Donald E. Stokes, *The American Voter* (New York: John Wiley & Sons, 1960); Peter W. Sperlich, *Human Affairs: A Study of Cross-Pressures and Political Behavior* (Chicago: Rand McNally & Co., 1971).

11. Robert Axelrod, "Where the Votes Come From: An Analysis of Electoral Coalitions, 1952-1968," *American Political Science Review*, Vol. 66, No. 1 (March 1972), p. 13.

12. Ibid., p. 17.

13. Everett Carll Ladd, Jr., *American Political Parties* (New York: W. W. Norton & Co., 1970), p. 269.

14. Ibid., p. 275

15. Mark R. Levy and Michael S. Kramer, *The Ethnic Factor: How America's Minorities Decide Elections* (New York: Simon & Schuster, 1972). This book gives a comprehensive account of ethnic voting in local, state, and national elections.

16. *Statistical Abstract of the United States, 1971*, No. 568, p. 365.

17. Kevin Phillips, *The Emerging Republican Majority* (New York: Arlington House, 1969). This book offers the thesis that ethnic groups are turning to the Republican Party. The notable exceptions are Jews and Blacks.

18. Raymond E. Wolfinger, "The Development and Persistence of Ethnic Voting," *American Political Science Review*, Vol. 59 (December 1965), pp. 896–908. Wolfinger argues that changes in economic status and geographic dispersion may reduce but will not eliminate ethnic feeling. His observations are largely based on the assumption that party loyalty will remain fairly static despite changes in lifestyle or issues of the day.

19. Phillips, *Emerging Republican Majority*, p. 461.

20. Ibid., pp. 469–70.

21. Ibid., p. 465.

5 Issues and Candidates

Presidential elections offer the American electorate an opportunity to choose their leaders and indirectly express opinions on the policies the candidates espouse. Voter perceptions of issues and candidates are closely related, but their relative impact on the voting decision is difficult to assess. Do voters cast their ballots for candidates they deem competent, or are political issues a more pervasive influence? There is doubtless a measure of both in the formulation of the voting decision. Consideration of this question will tell us much about the nature of Presidential elections and the political perceptions of the American voter.

ISSUES

Issues must be salient to an individual if they are to influence his political behavior. There are a variety of issues in any election campaign, and they are salient in varying degrees. Domestic issues are more likely to gain the attention of the voter because they directly affect his life. The price of food or the availability of gasoline strikes close to home. Most foreign policy issues, however, seem remote. The negotiation of an arms limitation treaty with the Soviet Union is not an issue that excites the electorate unless it becomes the source of partisan debate. Voters can form judgments on political issues only to the extent that they have sufficient information and interest. Without these two ingredients opinions are lightly held and unlikely to have an impact on voting behavior.[1]

Voter Perceptions

Voters must also perceive differences in the positions of candidates if issues are to affect voting behavior. For example, if both Presidential candidates endorse raising Social Security benefits, no issue is involved. But if one candidate advocates busing school children to achieve racial balance and his opponent favors a constitutional amendment to prohibit busing, the voter has a clear choice.

Presidential candidates usually reflect the prevailing sentiment of their parties. Early voting studies found that few voters discerned policy differences between the Democratic and Republican parties on most issues.[2] This view has been challenged in more recent research projects. The degree to which the electorate is able to differentiate between party positions on issues is a function of the choices they are presented.[3] If the parties blur rather than illuminate their own positions and fail to stress their differences with the opposition, the voter is left on his own. A study of the impact of the war in Vietnam on the 1968 election concluded that "The average American perceived Nixon and Humphrey as standing very close together on the escalation-deescalation dimension."[4] The political environment within which Presidential elections are held varies, and we would expect to find varying degrees of issue congruence and divergence between parties.

In addition to the impact of specific issues, the more general concerns of the public also influence election campaigns. Questions of whether the Democratic or Republican Party (or candidate) appears more capable in managing the economy or foreign affairs have an effect on voting behavior. In 1972, 1,288 persons of voting age were asked by the Survey Research Center: "Looking ahead, do you think that your family would get along better financially in the next four years if the Democrats or the Republicans win the election, or wouldn't it make much difference?" Twenty-three percent thought they would do better with the Democrats in power, 20 percent favored the Republicans in this respect, and 57 percent thought it would not make much difference. The same year, 1,245 persons asked by the Survey Center "Looking ahead, do you think the problem of keeping out of a bigger war would be handled better in the next four years by the Democrats, by the Republicans, or about the same by both?" responded as follows: better by Democrats, 15 percent; same by both, 54 percent; and better by Republicans, 31 percent.

These results are especially interesting because of the nature of the 1972 election, in which Nixon won reelection by a landslide. Although on broad issues of economic and foreign policy the majority of the electorate perceived the parties as being equally capable, over 60 percent of voters cast their ballots for Nixon. Data from previous elections show the same pattern.

Regardless of the victor or his margin, the electorate sees little difference in the ability of the parties to handle economic or foreign affairs. The relative importance of economic or foreign issues will vary, but the former is more relevant in most years.

The idea that most people "vote pocketbook" has been prevalent for many years, and there is much evidence to substantiate it. The 1942–52 era of Democratic domination was largely the result of New Deal economic policies which were perceived as a decided asset by the "working man." The nation's economy has changed, however, and the specter of depression no longer haunts American voters. The data in Chapter 4 gave evidence that the majority of the people have experienced a rapid improvement in their economic situation since the 1950s, and this improvement is expected to continue. Economic problems come to the fore today in a period of rapidly rising prices when real income is diminished. But, even if there is concern over the economy, it is unlikely to be interpreted in purely partisan terms. There is little difference in voter perceptions of the capabilities of the two parties in economic affairs. Pocketbook issues, once the dominant consideration in Presidential elections, must now share the spotlight with other issues.

The political life of the nation is dynamic, not static. Societal changes foster new areas of conflict and new issues. Robert M. Scammon and Ben J. Wattenburg, prominent political analysts, found that many social issues have come to the fore in the last decade. Racial integration has changed existing patterns of housing and led to controversy over school busing to achieve integration in education. There has been increased concern over "law and order." Supreme Court decisions in the Warren Court were viewed by many as putting law enforcement at a disadvantage vis-à-vis the lawbreaker, a trend the Nixon court has started to reverse. These Supreme Court decisions were rendered against a background of increasing crime and decreasing civility in American society. New challenges have arisen to the established order at all levels. The legitimacy of all our institutions, governmental and social, has declined in the view of most citizens. These social issues are not as clearly delineated as economic issues, and they add a new, unpredictable element in voting behavior.[5]

Problems and Issues

Table 5-1 shows the problems that were most important to the electorate prior to the 1968 and 1972 Presidential elections. Identifying problems is not the same as pinpointing election issues. As noted earlier in this chapter, voters saw little difference in the positions of Nixon and Humphrey on Vietnam in 1968. Scammon and Wattenburg point out that "a clear differentiation must be made between an *issue* and a *concern*. In 1968 . . . there was strong evidence to suggest that while the war was a paramount *concern*, it was not much of an *issue*. Each of the three candidates promised peace with honor."[6]

TABLE 5-1

MOST IMPORTANT PROBLEMS FACING NATION, 1968 AND 1972
(Percentage of respondents citing problems as most important)

Mid-October, 1968

Vietnam War...	44%
Crime (includes looting, riots)	25
Race relations...	17
High cost of living.......................................	6
Other problems, no opinion...............................	23

115%*

Late September, 1972

Vietnam War...	27%
Inflation, high cost of living.............................	27
Crime, lawlessness.......................................	8
International problems (general).........................	10
Drug use, abuse...	9
Other problems, don't know.............................	28

109%*

*Columns add to more than 100 percent because of multiple responses.
Source: Condensed from Gallup Polls.

This is an important distinction and one which relates to our consideration of economic issues. Voters must perceive a difference in the positions of candidates if national concerns are to be election issues.

Table 5-1 yields interesting insights into the extremely close Nixon-Humphrey election in 1968 and Richard Nixon's overwhelming victory over George McGovern in 1972. The Vietnam problem, as we have seen, was not viewed by the electorate in partisan terms in 1968. But the issues of crime and race relations — social issues — were viewed as problems by almost the same percentage of the electorate as viewed the war as a problem. George Wallace was the beneficiary of much of the protest vote on the social issues in the 1968 election, and this resulted in an extremely thin margin for Nixon. In contrast, the social issue did not come to the fore in 1972; inflation, Vietnam, and international problems were uppermost in voters' minds. It has been shown that the electorate sees little difference in the potential performance of either party in either the economic or international relations sphere. The first Nixon term had not witnessed inflammatory issues of sufficient force to overcome the inherent advantage of an incumbent in Presidential elections. If the Watergate story had unfolded before the election, the result might have been different. McGovern would have been provided with a salient issue.

What Is Salient?

The necessity for candidates to develop salient issues cannot be exaggerated. McGovern's appeals for minority rights and increased welfare payments were hardly the kinds of issues that create electoral majorities. Basically, he had no salient issue. The data indicate that the major issue in a Presidential contest involving an incumbent is the electorate's judgment on the performance of the administration in the preceding four years.[7] This does not negate the infusion of economic or foreign policy questions as salient issues in a campaign. An administration that took a Hoover-like hands-off approach to economic recession or rampant inflation would now surely suffer at the polls, but those in the White House know this. It is very unlikely that any President would rely solely on market forces to cure economic ills. A President who undertook an unpopular military adventure with great cost to the nation in terms of lives and money would seem a likely candidate for electoral retribution, but there is no evidence that Nixon's victory in 1968 rested on this issue. Rather, the urban riots in 1967 and 1968, a social issue, appear to have been the catalyst for Rebublican victory.

The resignation of Nixon and ascendancy of Gerald Ford to

the Presidency adds a new dimension to the 1976 election. Ford must succeed in separating his administration from the Watergate-related misdeeds of the Nixon White House if he is to win. His pardon of the former President makes this a formidable task. Government performance is salient to most voters—all but the extremely partisan—and it is unlikely that the Republicans will be rewarded at the polls. It appears to be an election that the Republicans cannot win, although the Democrats could lose with a candidate who is not viable or the creation of issues that go against the mainstream of political and social thought in the nation.

The rise of social issues has given an ideological tint to American parties, which heretofore have been marked by their lack of ideological fervor or programmatic approach. Both parties have been unduly influenced by their fringes—the right wing of the Republican Party and the left wing of the Democratic Party. McGovern's campaign was marked by an evangelical flavor. Opposition at the convention was effectively barred through a quota system which gave preference to representatives of minority groups, women, and the young. Writing before the 1972 convention, Scammon and Wattenburg prophetically state that the Democratic party and the left faction in particular must decide if they are a "movement" or a political party. They express it well:

> If it is a *movement,* convinced that there is but one shining truth that all right-thinking men must accept, then clearly the left must harass, disrupt, and coerce the party and the party's candidate toward its own viewpoint. . . . But if it is a *political party,* then what? A political party operates effectively between the two 35-yard lines of the political football field, wholly aware that there is a major substantative difference between one 35-yard line and the other, aware too that heading straight for the end zone leads to a political fumble.[8]

Scammon and Wattenburg go on to say that parties must "listen as well as lead." The passage above is as applicable to the Republican convention in 1964 that nominated Barry Goldwater as to the 1972 Democratic convention that nominated

McGovern. It is this brand of political evangelism that makes a
Watergate possible, if not probable. The rationale was summed
up by John Mitchell under questioning by the Senate Committee
investigating the Watergate affair. In answer to the question,
"Would you do anything necessary to ensure the election of the
President?" Mitchell replied: "Anything short of treason." The
most plausible explanation for the increased power of the fringes
of both parties is the interest in social issues, which rouse
passions to a greater degree than issues of foreign policy or the
economy.

Trends

The trend toward voting independency that we stressed in
Chapter 3 may be a result of the infusion of salient social issues
as well as the rise in income and education levels. Party loyalties
have weakened. The Republican Party, long regarded as elitist,
emerged from the 1968 and 1972 elections as the champion of
the blue-collar worker. The Democratic Party, forged by a coalition of minorities, ethnics, and blue-collar groups, is torn by the
obvious conflict between concern for minority rights and the
concern of segments of their coalition for maintenance of the
status quo.[9] The overwhelming desire of most citizens to retain

TABLE 5-2

PUBLIC'S PROFESSED POLITICAL PHILOSOPHY, 1972 AND 1967

	1972	1967	Percentage Change
Conservative	35%	38%	−3%
Middle of the road	34	37	−3
Liberal	19	14	+5
Radical	3	1	+2
Not sure	9	10	−1

Source: The Harris Survey, Nov. 27, 1972, © Chicago Tribune.

the familiarity of the status quo as opposed to the uncertainty associated with social change is documented in Table 5-2, which indicates the political labels respondents attach to themselves.

Sixty-nine percent of the 1972 respondents in Table 5-2 classify themselves as conservative or middle-of-the-road. The slight decline in these categories from the 1967 poll is probably due to the lessening of racial violence in the past few years, which has made racial tensions less visible though not less real. The groups most directly affected by increased efforts to achieve racial integration are the lower economic groups. The blacks in this group press for change and the whites resist, largely because they believe they will lose what the blacks gain. This explosive issue goes deeper than race, though this is the most prevalent device for explaining the conflict. Race provides a handle for the expression of hostility. The underlying issue is the desire of lower income groups for change and the resistance of those in the strata immediately above. The relevance of this issue in Presidential elections varies from being very salient to those most affected — the blue-collar worker — to diminishing degrees of saliency as one moves up the educational and income ladder.

Table 5-3 illustrates this point well. The self-perceptions of those with college educations tend to become increasingly liberal as their incomes increase. The largest shift in political philosophy, and probably the most significant one, is the increased liberalism of those under 30 years old. If this trend continues, the electorate will become increasingly liberal in the future. At the same time, those over 50 years old have grown more conservative.

The data in Table 5-3 indicate a liberal trend in the United States, which must be reconciled with political reality. Conservatives still outnumber liberals, with a large middle-of-the-road group. One reason is that groups within the Democratic coalition that are traditionally conservative were more interested in the economic benefits they felt the Democrats offered than with their professed liberal view toward minorities and the poor. This view is now perceived as posing a threat to the lifestyle of

TABLE 5-3
RELATIVE CHANGES IN POLITICAL PHILOSOPHY, 1967 to 1972

	Respondent-Self-Identification				
	Conser- vative	Middle Road	Lib- eral	Rad- ical	Not Sure
Groups Becoming More Liberal					
Total public					
1972	35%	34%	19%	3%	9%
1967	38	37	14	1	10
College educated					
1972	30	34	29	2	5
1967	40	41	13	1	5
Change	−10	− 7	+16	+ 1	—
Under 30					
1972	24	29	31	5	11
1967	38	40	11	2	9
Change	−14	−11	+20	+ 3	+ 2
Independent voters					
1972	30	34	23	4	9
1967	34	42	12	1	11
Change	− 4	− 8	+11	+ 3	− 2
$10,000 and over income					
1972	35	35	24	3	3
1967	39	43	12	1	5
Change	− 4	− 8	+12	+ 2	− 2
Groups Becoming Middle of the Road and Conservative					
South					
1972	40%	33%	12%	2%	13%
1967	43	26	17	1	13
Change	− 3	+ 7	− 5	+ 1	—
50 and over					
1972	42	36	11	2	9
1967	38	34	14	1	13
Change	+ 4	+ 2	− 3	+ 1	− 4
Republicans					
1972	53	31	8	1	7
1967	50	30	11	—	9
Change	+ 3	+ 1	− 3	+ 1	− 2

Source: The Harris Survey, Nov. 27, 1972 © Chicago Tribune.

conservative Democrats, which accounts for the disaffection of many traditionally Democratic voters. Large parts of the Democratic support have always come from conservative groups and areas—blue-collar workers, the Solid South. This did not have an impact on voting behavior until the pace of social change quickened and many Democrats felt more comfortable within Republican ranks. The Republicans, thus, were the beneficiary of this change.

The conservative-liberal split in the United States is not a clear-cut division along the lines of political ideology. A recent study of public opinion in this area concluded that the nation is conservative on such issues as reliance on individual initiative rather than on government, but it is liberal in its view of such social welfare programs as aid to education and housing.[10] The American public is thus conservative in its broad view toward the responsibilities of the individual for his own destiny but liberal in welcoming all the federal aid it can get. This contradiction must be considered by candidates seeking salient issues. The political folly of advocating programs that conflict with the ideological conservatism in the United States is exemplified in this passage from *Time* magazine the week before the 1972 election:

> By talking during the primary campaign of giving what his advisers called a $1,000 "demogrant" to everybody—even though the proposal was meant to replace some existing welfare programs—McGovern excited the social reformers, who are a minority in America, while deeply offending multitudes who thought it contradictory to the work ethic.[11]

There is evidence that issues have become increasingly important in Presidential elections as the electorate more correctly perceives party positions on issues regarded as salient.[12] There are relatively few such issues, and most fall into the social issue category. Increased public awareness dictates that candidates can profit more by responding to the concerns of the majority than by viewing Presidential elections as a crusade for the propagation of values which are antithetical to most voters.

CANDIDATES

It is difficult, if not impossible, to separate voter perceptions of Presidential candidates from their attitudes toward issues and parties. The emphasis placed upon the image of the candidate in determining election outcomes depends largely on one's view of the nature of Presidential elections. If one sees these contests as a collective judgment on the performance of the incumbent administration, the image of the candidates may be less important than campaign issues or party loyalty. But if Presidential elections are viewed as a projection of the electorate's judgment on the individual who can best lead the nation in the next four years, the image of the candidate is of prime importance.

Charisma and Competence

There are two sides to candidate imagery. One is the success of the candidate in projecting a picture of competence, a man who by virtue of experience and temperament is well equipped to serve. The other facet in candidate imagery is charisma, the projection of a dynamic, attractive personality. Obviously, the candidate who possesses the appearance of competence and has charismatic appeal will be tough to beat.

The relative importance of issues, candidates, and party varies in different campaigns. Many have seen Franklin Roosevelt as a master propagandist who was able to manipulate American public opinion through his "fireside chats." Though he was the first President to make extensive and very effective use of radio in seeking support for his policies, it is simplistic to attribute his four victories to personality factors. V. O. Key notes that "Even the most cursory reflection destroys this type of explanation in its crude form. . . .His position derived not so much from the kind of man he was as from the kinds of things for which, and against which, he fought."[13]

The victories of Dwight Eisenhower in 1952 and 1956 are explained by some in terms of his "father" image—a man you can trust. There is no doubt that he did benefit from the image of competence in foreign affairs. Little was known of his domestic opinions, but the fact that he defeated Robert Taft in the nomination served to separate him from old-guard Republican conservatism in economic matters. The favorable image of Eisenhower does not entirely explain his election, however, Key saw the election of 1952 as "more than plausibly characterized as a verdict of dissatisfaction with the past performance of the Democratic Administration."[14] This interpretation of the 1952 election diminishes the impact of Adlai Stevenson's image, whether it was good or bad. He was forced to run on the record of the Truman administration. This, in effect, was the prime issue in the election.

Studies which attempt to determine the relative importance of candidates and issues measure voter attitudes toward domestic and foreign affairs and relate them to voter assessment of the competence of a given candidate in each area. One study, which concluded that candidate charisma may well outweigh issues in some elections, contains this passage:

> It is hard today when Kennedy, in death, has wrung rivers of tears from an admiring world to recall the frame of mind of August 1960. Without the record created by public opinion polls we might easily rewrite history through the prism of later events that made of Kennedy the foreign-policy leader of the world. But the fact is that in August 1960, voters had little sense that Kennedy had any competence in international affairs. Insofar as they focused on foreign affairs, they were more inclined to favor Nixon.[15]

One could offer an alternate explanation for John Kennedy's victory that would be largely independent of the candidate. It is possible that after eight years of Republican rule and without the popular Eisenhower to head the ticket, the electorate was ready for a change.

It is important to remember in a discussion of Presidential candidates that the party leaders do not meet in convention to pick a loser. Most unsuccessful candidates for the Presidency have portrayed an aura of competence, if not charisma. There are two notable exceptions in the past ten years. The Republicans in 1964 and the Democrats in 1972 chose candidates who were out of the mainstream of American political thought. It is highly unlikely the Lyndon Johnson could have been defeated in 1964 or Nixon in 1972, since both enjoyed the tremendous advantage accruing to an incumbent President. However, it is probable that candidates who were less controversial could have avoided defeat of such proportions.

Nixon's landslide election has been attributed to causes ranging from confidence in Nixon to rejection of McGovern's views. Albert H. Cantrill and Charles W. Roll, Jr., conducted a study based on Gallup Poll data in an effort to determine the motivations for Nixon support.[16] This study yields insight into the 1972 election because it enables us to observe the impact of issues and candidates on the voting decision. Table 5-4 is the result of a question asking a selected sample of voters whether they were supporting their candidate "more because you especially like him and what he stands for, or more because you would hate to see the other man win."

This table offers a good view of voter motivation toward candidates and reveals a breakdown between the candidates that approximates the election results. Cantrill and Roll interpret Table 5-4 as a rejection of McGovern rather than an endorsement of Nixon or a rejection of McGovern's views. This conclusion is based on the fact that only 35 percent of Nixon's supporters "liked him." The data indicate that neither candidate attracted support based on personal popularity. If anything, Nixon's supporters were more enthusiastic about him than McGovern's were about their candidate. Of those who supported Nixon, about 60 percent "liked him," as opposed to less than 50 percent of McGovern's supporters. The 1972 Presidential election, then, appears to have rested on something other than the personal popularity of Nixon or the dislike of McGovern, although Nixon attracted a larger percentage of personal support. Responses to questions about candidates probably overemphasize the impact of candidate personality because Presidential candidates are the main reference point in elections, and responses are more likely to be directed to them

TABLE 5-4

REASONS FOR CANDIDATE SUPPORT IN 1972

Supported Nixon Because

Liked him	35%
Disliked McGovern	16
A little of both	9
	60%

Supported McGovern Because

Liked him	18%
Disliked Nixon	12
A little of both	10
	40%
Total opinion	100%

Source: Albert H. Cantrill and Charles W. Roll, Jr., published in *Philadelphia Inquirer*, December 17, 1972.

than to issues or parties.[17]

The Impact of Issues

Another indicator of the relationship between voter perceptions of issues and candidates is offered in Table 5-5. Early in October 1972, a cross section of 1,565 likely voters was asked: "If he were President, who do you think would be *(read off items on list)* — Nixon or McGovern?" This poll shows that Nixon had an average advantage over McGovern of about 10 percentage points when voters were asked which candidate could handle specific problems better. This is less than half of Nixon's electoral margin in the election. Again, this demonstrates the advantage that an incumbent enjoys in his reelection bid. He has had four years to build up an image of competence. This aura of experience looms larger in the judgment of most

TABLE 5–5

THE CANDIDATES AND THE ISSUES, 1972

	Nixon	McGovern	Not Sure
Better able to negotiate with Russians and Chinese	70%	14%	16%
More likely to move world closer to peace	57	26	17
Better able to keep inflation in check	55	27	18
More likely to end U.S. involvement in Vietnam sooner	48	35	17
Reduce unemployment quicker	44	34	22
Better in keeping corruption out of federal government	40	29	31
More likely to put in real tax reforms	35	43	22
Better in keeping big business from influencing federal government	32	43	25
More likely to cut defense spending	24	63	13
Average preference on nine issues			
Total voters	45	35	20
Union members	38	40	22
Big eight northern states	38	41	21
Under-30 voters	35	46	19

Source: The Harris Survey, Oct. 23, 1972, © *Chicago Tribune.*

voters than relative position on issues.

Charisma is a bonus attribute in Presidential candidates. Few, if any, have captured the imagination of the American public as did Kennedy. It is not essential that a candidate have this personal magnetism, however. Demonstrated experience or, lacking that, an appearance of competence appears to be the most significant quality of a Presidential aspirant. Voter perceptions of candidates are commingled with their ideas of the position of candidates on salient issues. The visibility of candidates leads many voters to say "I vote for the man, not the party," but this is an oversimplification of decision making in the voting choice. Some voters undoubtedly view the candidate as the embodiment of the party, while others refer to the candidate when they are really expressing their opinion of him as the symbol of an issue. No generalizations can be made about the relative importance of candidate and party. Each Presidential election is replete with its own characteristics, and the relative importance of candidates and issues will reflect the circumstances of the election.

NOTES

1. Philip E. Converse, "The Nature of Belief Systems in Mass Publics," in David E. Apter, ed., *Ideology and Discontent* (Glencoe, Ill.: Free Press, 1964), p. 251.

2. Angus Campbell, Philip E. Converse, Warren E. Miller, and Donald E. Stokes, *The American Voter* (New York: John Wiley & Sons, 1960), p. 182.

3. Gerald Pomper, "From Confusion to Clarity," *American Political Science Review*, Vol. 66 (June 1972), p. 427.

4. Benjamin I. Page and Richard A. Brody, "Policy Voting and the Electoral Process: The Vietnam War Issue," *American Politicial Science Review*, Vol. 66 (September 1972), p. 979.

5. Richard M. Scammon and Ben J. Wattenburg, *The Real Majority* (New York: Coward, McCann & Geoghegan, 1970), pp. 40–44.

6. Ibid., p. 307.

7. V. O. Key, Jr., with the assistance of Milton C. Cummings, Jr., *The Responsible Electorate* (New York: Vintage Books, 1968), p. 150.

8. Scammon and Wattenburg, *Real Majority*, pp. 317–18.

9. Richard W. Boyd, "Popular Control of Public Policy: A Normal Vote Analysis of the 1968 Election," *American Political Review*, Vol. 66, No. 2 (June 1972), pp. 429–49. This article details the emergence of social issues and the concomitant rise in ideology in Presidential elections. Also see in the same issue Richard A. Brody and Benjamin I. Page, "Comment: The Assessment of Policy Voting," pp. 450–58, and John H. Kessel, "Comment: The Issues in Issue Voting," pp. 459–65. An analysis of the impact of the Wallace candidacy in the 1968 election

is offered in Philip E. Converse, Warren E. Miller, Jerrold G. Rusk, and Arthur C. Wolfe, "Continuity and Change in American Politics: Parties and Issues in the 1968 Election," *American Political Science Review*, Vol. 63, No. 4 (December 1969), pp. 1083–1105.

10. Lester Markel, *What You Don't Know Can Hurt You* (Washington, D.C.: Public Affairs Press, 1972), p. 27. For a comprehensive study of public opinion, see Lloyd A. Free and Hadley Cantril, *The Political Beliefs of Americans* (New York: Simon & Schuster, 1968).

11. *Time Magazine*, October 30, 1972, p. 31.

12. Pomper, "From Confusion to Clarity."

13. Key, *Responsible Electorate*, p. 56.

14. Ibid., p. 75.

15. Ithiel de Sola Pool, Robert P. Abelson, and Samuel L. Popkin, *Candidates, Issues and Strategies* (Cambridge, Mass.: M.I.T. Press, 1964), p. 85.

16. Albert H. Cantrill and Charles W. Roll, Jr., *Philadelphia Inquirer*, December 17, 1972, p. 2–H.

17. See Jerrold G. Rusk and Herbert F. Weisberg, "Perceptions of Presidential Candidates: Implications for Electoral Change," *Midwest Journal of Political Science*, Vol. 16, No. 3 (August 1972), pp. 388–410.

6 Voting Patterns

The most common form of political participation in the United States is voting. It is impossible to assess the meaning and impact of Presidential elections without consideration of the voting patterns that emerge. Two dimensions are of primary interest. One is turnout—the percentage of voting-age population that casts a ballot in Presidential elections. Discussion of voting or nonvoting gives an insight into citizen interest or apathy. The other crucial dimension is the pattern of straight-ticket or split-ticket voting. This enables us to assess the impact of party loyalty. The political implications of an election are better understood through reference to such voting patterns.

VOTING AND NONVOTING

Voter turnout in Presidential elections since 1932 has ranged between approximately 52 and 63 percent. This is a source of concern to many observers who believe that the legitimacy of democratic government is weakened by lack of citizen participation. Comparisons are inevitably drawn between turnout in the

United States and other democracies; voting turnouts that exceed 90 percent are not uncommon in many nations. This disparity, however, is misleading. American statistics are based on the total voting-age population, while most nations base their voting figures on lists of eligible voters, a practice believed to exaggerate turnout by about 15 percent.[1] Some nations also mandate participation in elections with penalties for nonvoters.

Reasons for Nonvoting

The number of voting-age citizens who do not register to vote in the United States is sizable—about 33 million in 1972. Low registration has been ascribed to lengthy residency requirements in many states, but this explanation was largely eliminated by the Federal Voting Rights Act of 1970 which reduced to 30 days the residency required to vote for President and Vice-President.

There were about 12 million registered voters who did not vote in 1972. Almost half of this group was prevented from voting by difficult-to-surmount circumstances (Table 6–1). The group that could have voted but did not—about six million—is small compared to the 33 million who did not register.[2] It is to the latter group that we must look if the percentage of voting-age population participating in Presidential elections is to be increased.

TABLE 6–1

Reasons for Nonvoting   Given by Registered Voters, 1972 Presidential Election

Health reasons, no transportation, out of town, other unavoidable reasons	48%
Apathetic; dislike of politics, candidates, etc.	27
Other reasons or unknown reasons	25
	100%

Source: U.S. Department of Commerce, Bureau of the Census, *Current Population Reports,* Series P–20, No. 253, October 1973, p. 6.

Characteristics of Voters

Voting or nonvoting in Presidential elections appears to become a habitual part of an individual's political participation (or nonparticipation). Over three-quarters, or 78 percent, of the voting-age population reported consistent behavior in 1968 and 1972, either voting in both elections or voting in neither. Only 16 percent of the eligible voters reported voting in one election but not the other.

The relationship between education and voting behavior is striking. Of those with at least four years of college, 75 percent reported voting in both 1968 and 1972, while only 6 percent voted in neither. In contrast, the voting group with four years of education or less reported 30 percent voting in both, while 45 percent voted in neither 1968 nor 1972.

Table 6-2 shows the participation of key groups in the population in the Presidential elections of 1968 and 1972. The only one to increase the percentage voting in 1972 is the 18-20-year group, and this can be directly attributed to the enfranchisement of 18-year-old voters prior to the 1972 election. The relationship between education and voting is demonstrated by the fact that higher percentages of those with more education vote. It is a paradox that those groups that could conceivably benefit the most from an administration responsive to their needs tend to vote in lower percentages than the more advantaged citizens. Thus Negroes, the unemployed, and those with the lowest levels of education vote less than their contemporaries. Political participation, even in its most accessible and understandable form, evidently requires sufficient education to give it relevance. Note that the percentages reporting voting in 1968 and 1972 are about eight points higher than the actual turnout recorded in Table 6-3. This is due to overreporting of voting by individuals responding to interviews. The virtuous democratic citizen is expected to vote, and many individuals are unwilling to admit their failure to do so.

The rising levels of education in the United States observed in Chapter 4 would seem to herald an era of increased political

TABLE 6-2

PARTICIPATION IN NATIONAL ELECTIONS,
BY POPULATION CHARACTERISTICS, 1968-72

Characteristics	Percent Reporting They Voted	
	1968	1972
Male	69.8%	64.1%
Female	66.0	62.0
White	69.1	64.5
Negro	57.6	52.1
Age*		
18-20 years	33.3	48.3
21-24 years	51.1	50.7
25-34 years	62.5	59.7
35-44 years	70.8	66.3
45-64 years	74.9	70.8
65 and over	65.8	63.5
Residence		
Metropolitan	68.0	64.3
Nonmetropolitan	67.3	59.4
North and west	71.0	66.4
South	60.1	55.4
Education		
8 years or less	54.5	47.4
9-11 years	61.3	52.0
12 years	72.5	65.4
More than 12 years	81.2	78.8
Employment		
Employed	71.1	66.0
Unemployed	52.1	49.0
Not in labor force	63.2	59.3

*Covers civilian noninstitutional population 18 years old and over in Georgia and Kentucky, 19 and over in Alaska, 20 and over in Hawaii, and 21 years and older elsewhere in 1968.

Source: *Statistical Abstract of the United States, 1973*, No. 612. P. 379

interest and resultant larger percentages of Americans voting in Presidential elections. However, the data in Table 6–3 indicate that this has not been the case. A more informed electorate is not necessarily a more politically active one. Under the hypothesis that those with more information are more difficult to manipulate,[3] the decline in party loyalty observed in Chapter 3 could be expected to reduce the ability of the two major parties to produce heavy turnouts. Increased political awareness of the American electorate reduces party influence further.

A number of conclusions can be drawn from these data. First, the 1932 election took place in an atmosphere of fear and uncertainty generated by economic depression in which the struggle for subsistence apparently precluded increased political interest. Second, the myriad legislation that churned through Congress during Roosevelt's first term and perceptions of economic improvement resulted in a small increase in the 1936 turnout. Third, the stability of percentages voting in Presidential elections from 1932 to 1948 is striking in view of the variety of cataclysmic events that occurred in that period. Fourth, the failure of voting turnout to increase since 1952 is significant when one realizes that this period brought greatly increased voting by blacks who had been systematically deprived of their franchise in many Southern states. Fifth, the decrease in percentages voting in the 1972 election may be explained by the enfranchisement of 18-year-olds for the first time on a national basis. Table 6–2 above shows that the percentage of this age group that reported voting in 1972 is lower than that for older groups of voters.

We have also seen that voting—or nonvoting—tends to form a stable pattern. It represents a habit of political participation or nonparticipation. The turnout in contests for the House of Representatives illustrates the degree of political apathy in the United States; less than half of the voting-age population has voted in any off-year Congressional election since 1932. These elections do not attract the level of media exposure or general interest that attends Presidential elections. This is due both to the lack of visibility of most House members and the abdication

TABLE 6-3

**VOTER PARTICIPATION IN ELECTIONS FOR PRESIDENT
AND U.S. REPRESENTATIVES, 1932-72**

Year	President	U.S. House of Representatives
1932	52.4%	49.7%
1934	—	41.4
1936	56.9	53.5
1938	—	44.0
1940	58.9	55.4
1942	—	32.5
1944	56.0	52.7
1946	—	37.1
1948	51.1	48.1
1950	—	41.1
1952	61.6	57.6
1954	—	41.7
1956	59.3	55.9
1958	—	43.0
1960	62.8	58.5
1962	—	46.1
1964	61.8	58.1
1966	—	45.4
1968	60.9	55.2
1970	—	43.5
1972	55.7	51.0

Note: Percentages based on voting-age population.

Source: Statistical Abstract of the United States, 1973, No. 611. P. 379.

of power by Congress since 1932. Clearly, visibility of Congressmen is a function of Congressional activity and influence.

Participation Trends

What degree of political participation can we expect in future elections? An increasing number of Americans have the evaluative tools to form reasoned political judgments, and this has resulted in a decrease of party loyalty. However, increased awareness does not automatically lead to increased voting. Only political events of sufficient magnitude can stir the citizenry to the realization that their vote does count and they do have a choice in the manner in which they are governed. The depression of the 1930s and international conflicts since World War II have not provided this stimulus because, we hypothesize, most Americans have tended to view these events in nonpartisan terms. It was demonstrated in Chapter 5 that most voters see little difference in the ability of the two major parties to deal with economics or foreign affairs. The prime issue in Presidential elections appears to be a judgment of the performance of incumbent administrations.

The events surrounding the Watergate affair may well prove a watershed in American politics. Clearly, the public is aroused by the excesses of the Executive branch of government. The awe and respect of the Presidency have been diminished. It is possible that an increasingly well-educated electorate will come to the conclusion that their vote does make a difference and is the only effective bar to government excess. The 1976 Presidential election will be a test of this notion. It is difficult to foresee a series of events which could do more to spur increased voting than those involving political activities of the Nixon administration.

TICKET-SPLITTING

Several possible factors motivate voters to cast their ballots for the Presidential candidate of one party and for senators or representatives of the opposition. The voter may respond to state or local issues and candidates independently of his judgment of Presidential issues and candidates. Or he may have a strong emotional tie to one party at the local level but fail to carry this allegiance to national candidates. There is also the possibility of voters responding to a type of ballot which encourages (or at least does not discourage) the split ballot. Since states are responsible for voting laws, different types of ballots are used in Presidential elections.

A study of the 1956 election emphasized the different types of ballots found in various states.[4] Twenty-six states facilitated straight-party voting by allowing votes cast for one party to be registered by pulling a single lever. In other states the Presidential vote was separated from the balance of the ballot, thus requiring two or more decisions. There were other variations, but none obviated the possibility of voting a straight ticket. The effect of the type of ballot on voting behavior is pronounced. In 1956 59 percent of Eisenhower voters in single-choice states voted straight Republican, compared to 48 percent in states where several choices had to be made. Sixty-nine percent of Stevenson supporters voted a straight ticket in single-choice states, compared to 60 percent in multiple-choice states. Thus some but by no means all ticket-splitting can be attributed to the form of ballot. The form of the ballot makes ticket-splitting easier but does not cause it, unless voters erroneously split their vote.

Evidence of ticket-splitting can be found by examining the results of Congressional and Presidential races over a period of time. Table 6–4 relates the impact of success in Presidential elections on Congressional races held in those years. In 1932, obviously a pivotal year in American politics, over one-fifth of the seats in the House of Representatives changed from Republican to Democratic. This is a far greater change in party alignment than would be expected given the size of Roosevelt's victory. Over one-third of the Senate seats at stake also changed parties; with only 32 seats at stake, the Democrats realized a gain of 12.

Note that in 1936, Franklin Roosevelt increased his percentage of the popular vote, but the accompanying Democratic gains in Congress were modest. Not until 1948 was there another Presidential election in which there was also a sizable shift in party strength in Congress. This is explained not as a dramatic shift to the Democratic Party but as a recapturing of seats lost in the off-year elections.

The small changes in relative party strength in 1952 and 1956 are interesting: Dwight Eisenhower's popularity obviously did not rub off on Republican congressional candidates. Nor did Richard Nixon's victories in 1968 and 1972 succeed in giving the Republican Party control of either the House or the Senate. There is no evidence that the size of Nixon's plurality in 1972

TABLE 6-4

CONGRESSIONAL GAINS AND LOSSES, 1932-72

Year	House Gains/Losses Demo-cratic	House Gains/Losses Repub-lican	Senate Gains/Losses Demo-cratic	Senate Gains/Losses Repub-lican	President	% of Popular Vote
1932	+97	−101	+12	−12	(D) Roosevelt	57.4%
1934	+ 9	− 14	+10	−11		
1936	+11	− 14	+ 6	− 8	(D) Roosevelt	60.8
1938	−71	+ 80	− 6	+ 6		
1940	+ 5	− 7	− 3	+ 5	(D) Roosevelt	54.7
1942	−45	+ 47	− 9	+10		
1944	+21	− 19	0	0	(D) Roosevelt	53.4
1946	−55	+ 56	−12	+13		
1948	+75	− 75	+ 9	+ 9	(D) Truman	49.6
1950	−29	+ 28	− 6	+ 5		
1952	−21	+ 22	− 1	+ 1	(R) Eisenhower	55.1
1954	+19	− 18	+ 1	− 1		
1956	+ 2	− 2	+ 1	0	(R) Eisenhower	57.4
1958	+49	− 47	+17	−13		
1960	−20	+ 20	− 2	+ 2	(D) Kennedy	49.5
1962	− 4	+ 2	+ 4	− 4		
1964	+38	− 38	+ 2	− 2	(D) Johnson	61.1
1966	−47	+ 47	− 3	+ 3		
1968	− 4	+ 4	− 5	+ 5	(R) Nixon	43.4
1970	+12	− 12	− 4	+ 2		
1972	−13	+ 13	+ 2	− 2	(R) Nixon	60.8

signaled anything more than a vote of confidence in his administration. If 1972 truly marked a shift in party power, we would
expect to see the type of Republican gains in Congress that the
Democratic Party enjoyed in 1932.

Impact of Ticket-Splitting on Party Strength

Table 6–4 gives evidence that the electorate does not equate
the Presidency with Congressional candidates. The stability of
party identification and its impact on voting behavior appears to
be quite meaningful if we restrict its importance to Congressional races. There does not appear to be a substantial carry-over of
party loyalty to Presidential candidates, who often run completely independent campaigns and make little effort to help
their party candidates. An excellent example of this circum-
stance was Nixon's 1972 campaign; he made virtually no effort
to aid other Republicans. In any event, Presidential candidates
who have attempted to influence Congressional contests have
been largely unsuccessful. The different character of Presidential and Congressional elections is one of the best documented
facts in American political life.

The voting patterns in off-year elections illustrated in Table
6–4 are significant to an understanding of voting behavior in
American politics. The only off-year election in the 40-year
period included in Table 6–4 in which an incumbent President's
party increased its representation in the House of Representatives was 1934. The picture in the Senate is slightly different.
Off-year elections in 1934, 1946, 1962, and 1970 resulted in
the incumbent's party gaining seats in the Senate, although the
gain in the latter two years was minimal.

Changes in the makeup of Congress that occur during off-year
elections appear to be a return to a balance of political power
which reflects party strength. The balance is somewhat altered
in Presidential election years by a coat-tail effect which favors
Congressional candidates of the victorious party. While, as
stated earlier, this influence is not always strong, it is consistently evident. We thus observe a pendulumlike movement

between the two major parties which usually results in Congressional gains for the party that captures the Presidency but inevitable losses for that party in the following Congressional election.

It is the relative size of these gains and losses that reflects the strength of the Congressional parties at any given time. Since 1952 there has been consistent Democratic control of Congress, despite four Republican victories in the past six Presidential elections. Only in 1946 and 1952 did the Republicans gain control of the House and Senate, and they lost 45 House and 13 Senate seats during the Eisenhower administration. The Democrats fared a little better during the Kennedy-Johnson years; they lost 33 seats in the House but gained 1 in the Senate. Nixon's two victories were accompanied by Republican gains of five seats in both houses of Congress. If the trend we have observed continues, these gains will likely be erased in 1974.

Table 6-5 shows the party composition of Congress since 1932. How do we reconcile the persistence of Democratic control of Congress despite Republican Presidential successes? Political parties appear to be more salient in Congressional elections than in contests for the Presidency. The persistent stability of party identification that was noted in Chapter 3 bears a striking similarity to Democratic majorities in Congress during most of the past 40 years. The Democratic Party has been unable, however, to tap this residue of party loyalty to maintain control of the White House. The electorate apparently views Presidential elections as political events beyond the parties themselves. Voting decisions are obviously made in response to issues and candidates rather than simply as a reflection of party identification. In contrast, Congressional elections come close to approximating the division of party strength as measured by indices of party identification.

The voting pattern we have observed is evidence of substantial ticket-splitting. There are many ways in which ballots can be divided among political parties. The most common split is to vote for the Presidential and Vice-Presidential candidates of one party and at least one Congressional candidate of the other party. It is this type of ballot that explains the divergent patterns seen in Tables 6-4 and 6-5.

Historically, most American voters were straight-ticket voters. A recent study by Walter DeVries and Lance Terrance, Jr., *The Ticket-Splitter,* estimates that less than 20 percent split their ballots before World War II. This party regularity has decreased dramatically since that time. Several reasons are advanced to explain this change:

The decrease in straight party voting in the late 1960's is associated with the weakening of old-line party organizations and spe-

TABLE 6-5

PARTY DIVISION IN CONGRESS, 1932-72

Year	House		Senate	
	Democratic	Republican	Democratic	Republican
1932	313	117	59	36
1934	322	103	69	25
1936	333	89	75	17
1938	262	169	69	23
1940	267	162	66	28
1942	222	209	57	38
1944	243	190	57	38
1946	188	246	45	51
1948	263	171	54	42
1950	234	199	48	47
1952	213	221	47	48
1954	232	203	48	47
1956	234	201	49	47
1958	283	154	66	34
1960	263	174	64	36
1962	258	176	68	32
1964	295	140	67	33
1966	248	187	64	36
1968	243	192	58	42
1970	255	180	54	44
1972	242	193	56	42

cial-interest group leaders. . . . The decline in the brokerage power of political organization leaders, of professional, business, and
labor groups, of educational groups, and even of strong religious
and ethnic organizations reflects the spread of voter independence and estrangement from strong organizational ties and
bloc-vote commitments.[5]

Some may disagree with the conclusions of the authors of *The
Ticket-Splitter* with regard to the diminishing importance of ethnic and religious bloc voting. But there is no doubt that ticket-splitting has increased since World War II and shows every
indication of continuing to do so. The trend between 1960 and
1968 illustrated in Table 6-6 reflects a move away from party
regularity and is in keeping with the voting patterns observed in
Tables 6-4 and 6-5. A Gallup Poll taken shortly after the 1972

TABLE 6-6

STRAIGHT- AND SPLIT-TICKET VOTING, 1960-68
(Including state and local elections in Presidential years)

1960	
Voted straight Democratic	40.9%
Voted straight Republican	32.0
Split ticket	27.1
No. of cases—1,390	100.0%
1964	
Voted straight Democratic	42.3%
Voted straight Republican	17.3
Split ticket	40.4
No. of cases—981	100.0%
1968	
Voted straight Democratic	28.7%
Voted straight Republican	22.7
Split ticket	48.6
No. of cases—990	100.0%

Source: Survey Research Center.

TABLE 6-7

ANALYSIS OF 1968 VOTE BY STRAIGHT OR SPLIT TICKETS

	Straight Ticket	Split Ticket	Don't Know
National	43%	54%	3%
Sex			
Men	43	55	2
Women	43	53	4
Race			
White	42	55	3
Nonwhite	—	—	—
Education			
College	34	64	2
High school	40	58	2
Grade school	61	34	5
Occupation			
Professional & Business	35	62	3
White collar	35	63	2
Farmers	43	54	3
Manual labor	44	53	3
Age			
21-29 years	32	66	2
30-49 years	39	59	2
50 & over	50	46	4
Religion			
Protestant	44	53	3
Catholic	43	53	4
Jewish	—	—	—
Politics			
Republican	53	45	2
Democrat	49	47	4
Independent	25	72	3
Region			
East	46	50	4
Midwest	41	57	2
South	43	53	4

West	40	58	2
Income			
$10,000 & over	38	60	2
$ 7,000 & over	38	60	2
$ 5,000–$6,999	41	53	6
$ 3,000–$4,999	50	48	2
Under $3,000	57	37	6
Community size			
1,000,000 & over	49	49	2
500,000 & over	49	49	2
50,000–499,999	41	57	2
2,500–49,999	39	56	5
Under 2,500, rural	39	57	4

Source: The Gallup Opinion Index, December 1968, Report No. 42.

election indicates that approximately 60 percent of the electorate split their tickets.

The 1972 election offers an insight into the increased pattern of ticket-splitting in Presidential election years. It was the first time a President was elected with more than 60 percent of the popular vote, but his party failed to add seats in the House and Senate. And it was also the only instance in which such a resounding victory failed to give the winning candidate's party a majority in both Houses of Congress. The failure of Nixon's victory to materially aid Republican Congressional candidates extended to gubernatorial contests, in which Democrats won 11 of the 18 seats that were up for election.[6]

Table 6–7 gives insight into the characteristics of voters who voted split and straight tickets in 1968. Those surveyed were asked: "For the various political offices, did you vote for all the candidates of one party—that is, a straight ticket—or did you vote for the candidates of different parties?" The majority of those with more education split their tickets, as did those in the higher income groups. Independents, as expected, split their tickets more than party identifiers, but almost half of the latter group also voted for candidates of different parties. Younger voters were more prone to split their tickets than were older voters. The data do not indicate how many voted a straight ticket because of conviction rather than habit. The potential number of ticket-splitters is obviously higher than the observable percentages in a given election.

Rising levels of income and education may be expected to bring increased ticket-splitting. There is every reason to believe that the American voter has become increasingly sophisticated in his voting decision making. He is demonstrating by steadily increasing percentages the ability and desire to sift through candidates at various levels of government and make choices based on the exigencies of a particular race. As noted earlier, the impact of party is greater at the local and state level, and it has not been translated into consistent party loyalty for Presidential candidates. The steady increase in ticket-splitting is a result.

NOTES

1. William H. Flanigan, *Political Behavior of the American Electorate* (Boston: Allyn & Bacon, 1968), p. 15.

2. Ibid., pp. 5-6.

3. Ibid., p. 18. Flanigan also observes that "Currently in Europe it is correct to say that the higher the interest in and information on politics in the nation generally, the lower the turnout in elections."

4. Angus Campbell and Warren E. Miller, "The Motivational Basis of Straight and Split Ticket Voting," *American Political Science Review*, Vol. LI, No. 2, June 1957, pp. 293-312.

5. Walter De Vries and Lance Terrance, Jr., *The Ticket-Splitter* (Grand Rapids, Mich.: William B. Eerdmans Publishing Co., 1972), pp. 22-23.

6. *Congressional Quarterly*, February 23, 1974, p. 440.

7 Presidential Election Campaign Techniques

The declining effectiveness of political party organizations has brought about tremendous change in the planning and execution of Presidential election campaigns. The professional campaign organization, skilled in the use of mass media, has replaced the party cadres, whose forte was effective person-to-person persuasion. Presidential hopefuls today seek nomination through their own campaign organizations and, if successful, depend upon them for the election campaign.

Traditionally, candidates exhorted the electorate to remain loyal to their party and invoked the names of party notables to rouse their audiences. Modern campaigns are waged with little emphasis on party. Candidates depend instead on their ability to portray an aura of competence and to offer programs which are capable of capturing the imagination and attention of the electorate. Robert Agronoff notes the tendency of campaigns and strategies to be independent of parties:

> The style and technology of campaigning blends well with this independence. Indeed, it simultaneously supports it and produces it. Changes in the habits of the American voters, the rapid growth

in the size of constituencies, new means of communication and the application of new technologies have caused a virtual revolution in campaigning which in turn is accelerating the change in the entire political fabric of America.[1]

This passage succinctly points up the impact of lessening party loyalties which we have observed in preceding chapters on the process of electing a President. Increasing voter independence of party, based upon a better educated citizenry, is coupled with increased accessibility to political news through the mass media. It is this combination of events which reinforce each other that has led to the new-style Presidential election campaign.

CAMPAIGN STRATEGY

The overall strategies formulated by candidates to guide their campaigns are predicated upon assumptions about the mood and composition of the electorate. Information about the electorate helps to determine the types of issues to be stressed and the kind of image the candidate should project. Taking into account the composition of the electorate, broken down in terms of groups based on issues or socioeconomic characteristics, permits the strategy to be based on expected reactions of large groups of voters. The strategist who draws detailed campaign plans also must be aware of the importance of flexibility and the ability to respond to new challenges. Events occur in the course of campaigns that were unforeseen and require shifts in strategy, and plans must be altered to take advantage of unexpected areas of strength or bolster those of apparent weakness.

Several basic decisions are the foundation of any Presidential campaign. What is the best approach to the electorate? Should a candidate vigorously attack the opposition or attempt to run on selected issues? What type of organization should be formed—one based on existing party apparatus or an independent structure formed for the campaign? How much money can be counted on? This will have an obvious impact on strategy. What are the pivotal states? This requires an assessment of the candidate's strength in states with large electoral votes and determines where it is most profitable to spend time and money.

The answers to these questions are affected by whether a candidate is an incumbent or challenger. The former has a better idea of both his potential support and sources of funds. An incumbent also is tied by events to certain issues — war, recession, and corruption are a few examples. The challenger has the task of attacking administration failures as well as offering programs for a better tomorrow. We shall examine the options available in arriving at an overall campaign strategy, mindful of the characteristics of the American electorate observed in the preceding chapters.

THE CAMPAIGN ORGANIZATION

Presidential campaigns are traditionally the rallying point for the party faithful on all levels of organization. In the past, the national committee of each party assumed the principal responsibility for devising strategy and coordinating the efforts of the multitudinous party organizations. The task of raising money to finance campaigns fell to party notables at every level. Local party organizations attempted to contact voters personally to solicit their support. Party effort thus reached from the national committee to ward leaders, precinct captains, and committeemen.

Today campaign responsibility has shifted from the national committees to a candidate-controlled and professionally staffed organization. Increased emphasis on television has made it necessary to rely on individuals skilled in the use of this media. Conventional political wisdom has been replaced by scientific polling, which is better accomplished by pollsters than politicians. The ability of the political organization to deliver the vote also has come into question. Two Republican victories with Dwight Eisenhower heading the ticket are ample proof that,

TABLE 7-1

PERCENTAGE OF VOTERS CONTACTED BY PARTY WORKERS, MID-OCTOBER, 1968

	Yes— Personal Call	Yes— Telephoned	Neither	Don't Remember
Democrat	6%	2%	91%	1%
Republican	8	4	88	1

Source: The Gallup Opinion Index, November, 1968, Report No. 41.

party identification notwithstanding, virtually all areas of the nation and all segments of the electorate are worth cultivating.

Table 7-1 offers a glimpse of the level of local party activity in the 1968 election. Respondents were asked: "In this election campaign has any Democratic (Republican) party worker called upon you personally or telephoned to try to get you to vote for Democratic (Republican) candidates?" The low level of party activity evidenced in Table 7-1 is only partially explained by the fact that the poll was taken about three weeks before the election, and doubtless more contacts were made in this period. It nevertheless indicates that both local Democratic and Republican organizations were something less than zealous in the six weeks following the traditional Labor Day beginning of national campaigns. The question asked did not differentiate on whose behalf voters were contacted.

Local party workers often have more interest in local or Congressional races than in the Presidential election. The committeeman can hardly expect recognition from a successful Presidential candidate, but he may receive tangible political rewards from candidates on a local level. It is apparent that Presidential candidates who place their primary dependence upon local party activity are doomed to defeat.

The national party organizations are usually controlled by the candidates. Given the permanent nature of the organizations, they can offer a valuable auxiliary service to professional campaign managers. Both parties have developed computerized records of contributors and possible campaign workers at all levels, a project of obvious worth. A recent study of national party campaign activity reached this conclusion:

> Contemporary party involvement in the new campaigning can best be described as evolutionary and peripheral. In most cases, central organizations are involved only in fragments of management, information and media. The services they offer generally have very little to do with the day-to-day management of the campaign or with the making of key campaign decisions.[2]

The national committees do render important assistance to Congressional candidates unable to afford the array of expertise required for modern campaigns. However, the desire of Presidential candidates to have complete control of their campaigns and the necessity of a major fund-raising effort solely on behalf of the aspirant for the White House have led to the formation of campaign organizations outside the influence of the national party. The Presidential candidate thus has his personal organization for planning and implementing campaign strategy and such services of the national committee as he chooses to use.

Professional campaign organizations devoted exclusively to this pursuit date back to 1935.[3] The hallmark of early efforts to professionalize campaigning, which continues in contempory organizations, is the tactic of going directly to the voter, thus circumventing the party.

The 1952 race was the first in which television played an important role. Most of the populous areas of the nation could be reached by this medium by the time of the election, but there were only 19 million TV receivers. The Eisenhower campaign staff was well supplied with advertising and public relations experts, but few were brought into the campaign solely for their expertise. Most had been active politically and were more or less considered regular members of the party team.[4] Included in the latter group were advertising executives who had worked for Thomas E. Dewey in 1948 and other Republican campaigns, so the 1952 election was not the first in which media experts played an important role. The Republican campaign was marked by the dominance of the campaign organization, brought together for one Presidential election, over the established party apparatus. In contrast, Adlai Stevenson used advertising agencies to help plan media exposure, and the campaign organization was dominated by those who had held public relations posts in government or the news media.[5]

THE PROFESSIONALS AND THE MEDIA

> Hail to B.B.D. & O.
> It told the nation how to go:
> It managed by advertisement
> To sell us a new President.
>
> Eisenhower hits the spot
> One full general, that's a lot.
>
> Feeling sluggish, feeling sick?
> Take a dose of Ike and Dick.
>
> Philip Morris, Lucky Strike,
> Alka Seltzer, I like Ike.[6]

This ditty, written in 1952, symbolizes the view that Presidents can be sold like cigarettes or bromide. In many ways, this view has become a self-fulfilling prophecy. Campaign managers believe it and therefore surround themselves with public relations types. It is, of course, impossible to determine the extent to which campaign advertising actually determines the final outcome. Communication is the crux of campaigning, and it is certainly prudent to make use of experts in this area. But Presidential campaigns hinge on more than imagery or other public relations techniques. Elections are held within a political milieu that is impossible to brush aside. For instance, it is unlikely that public relations efforts on behalf of the Republican candidate in 1976 will succeed in selling General Haig's "devil theory" to the electorate as an explanation for White House tape erasures. The increasingly well-educated public that is the target of such efforts has the evaluative tools to form reasoned judgments.

Attention to specific areas of professional campaign management will help place the advertising aspect of Presidential campaigns in perspective. Not all media coverage is paid advertising. Presidential candidates are accompanied by representatives of the press, radio, and television during all their waking moments and receive media exposure which results in recognition by all segments of the electorate. This is due to the visibility of the Presidency, not the acumen of campaign managers. Careful planning, however, helps create favorable situations for media coverage.

Nixon's 1968 campaign employed the strategy of having the candidate's appearances at public events scheduled early enough in the day to allow television coverage on the 6:00 o'clock news. Melvyn Bloom notes that election campaigns are more concerned with exposure than substance:

> Since television is the way you get to most voters, the reasoning went, public events are not held for reasons of content or validity, but mainly to provide television with something to report. . . . The events themselves and the audiences that turned out for them might be largely irrelevant at times.[7]

The Nixon approach also featured televised appearances before selected panels of reportedly friendly people. The questions were seldom pointed, the questioners seldom abrasive, and Richard Nixon had an excellent showcase to display a confident, capable candidate.[8] This kind of appearance shielded Nixon from confrontations with the press; he was clearly not at his best in free-wheeling exchanges with reporters. The entire television strategy rested on the premise that voters will judge the image they see rather than the individual behind the image. In contrast to Nixon's 1960 campaign in which he emphasized his fulfillment of a pledge to campaign in all 50 states, the 1968 campaign was marked by a relatively leisurely pace, with no effort to tax Nixon's endurance in a hectic whirl of public appearances. Television was the major thrust of the Republican 1968 campaign.

Hubert Humphrey's 1968 campaign was also planned largely as an exercise in the use of TV. Joseph Neopolitan, one of his

key advisors, stressed that exposure is not always beneficial. It must be used in a positive manner or it will be counter-productive.

> You lose them when you put your guy in front of a camera, the kind, you know, where he starts out, "Good evening ladies and gentlemen, my name is Joe Blow and I want to talk to you about taxes." When you do that you can hear the click of sets being switched or turned off all over the state.[9]

The Humphrey campaign suffered from lack of money, especially at the outset. While some have blamed his narrow defeat on this handicap, the point is debatable. Humphrey was an incumbent Vice-President who had voter recognition from years in the limelight. Television exposure, like any form of public relations effort, reaches a point of diminishing return.

The 1972 election campaigns differed procedurally but not in overall strategy. Both candidates formed their own professional staffs rather than relying on advertising agencies. This was more to tighten control than for any other purpose. McGovern's problems epitomize the dilemma of a challenger running against an incumbent President. Nixon could point to an accommodation with Red China and the winding down of our involvement in Vietnam, and the economy was in fairly good shape. Only Watergate threatened to be a fly in the ointment, but the extent of White House involvement had not been verified at the time of the election, and many did not place importance on the event. On the other hand, the Eagleton episode gave George McGovern a poor start in his bid for the Presidency. When he shifted from "1000 percent support" to asking Thomas F. Eagleton to step aside as his running mate for the Vice-Presidency, the indecisiveness with which he handled this matter projected an image McGovern could never overcome.

This points to another limitation in the use of media. Actions of a candidate during a campaign which cast doubt on his potential for leadership cannot be repaired by public relations efforts. Only time can ameliorate, if not erase, unfavorable public impressions of political figures.

Television is not without its limitations. The most important is the inability to choose the audience, except in the broadest terms, which makes it difficult to address the issues because of fear of offending a segment of the viewers. TV-centered campaigns must be devoted to building the candidate's image as a man worthy of the office. Exposure was indispensable to John Kennedy in 1960. His efforts to establish himself in the public view as a serious, responsible candidate were aided greatly by the televised debates with Nixon, which gave him a visibility he had not heretofore achieved and an image vital to his chances for election.

Television is not the sole medium of campaign public relations efforts. Radio, which had been the standby of Roosevelt, was given new emphasis in 1972. The Committee for the Re-election of the President prepared a series of five-minute commercials which were widely disseminated, as well as 60-second spots attacking McGovern's positions and capacity for leadership. It is difficult to judge whether the sizable sums of radio spending are a reflection of its potential in Presidential elections, despite the emphasis on television, or the result of the need to spend enormous sums of money to justify soliciting the contributions.

Direct mail was used in 1972 in unprecedented quantities. Efforts of the McGovern organization were largely directed at solicitation of campaign funds. Bloom notes that "The results astonished even the McGovern optimists, as the direct mail campaign brought in as much as $850,000 in a single mid-October day."[10] The Nixon campaign also utilized direct mail. Personally addressed appeals for support were sent to between 10 and 15 million voters in key states. The purpose of this massive effort was more to solicit votes than to ask for contributions.

What is the impact of the media on the electorate in terms of influencing voting decisions? The candidates gain the nomination after a long, arduous primary struggle which also receives intense media coverage. This exposure is capped by televised convention proceedings. There is no such thing as an "unknown" emerging from the conventions. Recognition, then, is not the basic reason for media campaigns. Rather, the media offers the best way to reach the largest audience in the least time in an effort to project a favorable image of the candidate.

Table 7-2 gives some idea of the percentage of the electorate whose choice before the campaign got underway remained firm until election time. The most revealing element in Table 7-2 is the similarity between voter preference before the start of the campaign and the final result. In the 1964 election Johnson actually received about 61 percent of the vote, so the undecideds went en masse to Goldwater. The early polls in 1968 are less indicative of the outcome. The candidacy of George Wallace is a factor in underreporting of Nixon-Humphrey strength. Polls taken two weeks before the election are close to the one

TABLE 7-2

VOTER CHOICE AT EARLY STAGES OF CAMPAIGN, 1964-72

1964 — Postconvention	
Goldwater	31%
Johnson	61
Undecided	8
1968 — August 24	
Nixon	40%
Humphrey	34
Wallace	17
Undecided	9
1972 — August	
Nixon	57%
McGovern	34
Undecided	8

Source: Harris Survey, *The Washington Post,* July 22, 1964; *New York Post,* November 1, 1968; 1972 Chicago Tribune-New York News Syndicate, October 22, 1972.

shown in the table, with Humphrey picking up 2 percent from the undecideds and 1 percent from Wallace. Splitting the undecided vote in 1972 between Nixon and McGovern yields approximately the percentages each candidate received in the election.

The data obscure changes within all the groups, but the overall percentages lead to the hypothesis that much campaign spending is wasted. In 1972 Nixon gained nothing, despite an outlay estimated at about $70 million, almost double the McGovern expenditures. The 1964 figures also are within sampling error of the election result.[11] A convincing argument can be made that in close elections — such as 1968 — the effect of media efforts is crucial. But, as Neopolitan pointed out, poor use of media can be harmful. The effectiveness of media efforts cannot be measured in terms of dollars and cents.

POLLS AND STRATEGY

Polling has become a prime tool in the arsenal of campaign strategists. Polls can be used to ascertain the issues that are most important to the electorate and to determine which of several possible alternatives is likely to be most palatable. This enables a candidate to concentrate his efforts on salient issues and avoid the peripheral ones.

Polls on hot issues that arise during a campaign should be allowed to ripen before drawing conclusions and possibly altering campaign strategy. Dramatic news events may produce a short-lived reaction that is not indicative of the underlying public mood. It is essential for campaign managers to identify correctly the predispositions of the electorate. Media campaigns have limitations in that they cannot place issues in the public mind and make them salient. Intelligent use of polls can highlight issues that are relevant and suggest viable approaches, but poll information does not in itself dictate any particular course of action to a candidate. Charles W. Roll, Jr., and Albert H. Cantrill note that the candidate has three choices when he finds his view on an issue differs from public opinion: "He can persist and try to persuade the public to his view; he can side-step the issue; or he can follow the public consensus."[12]

The strategy employed by a candidate is in part dependent on how strongly, if at all, he has expressed his views on a particular issue. It is difficult to change an oft-stated position for the sake of conforming to public opinion, but this can be done with relatively low-key statements. It is a mistake to view Presidential election campaigns as an opportunity to educate the electorate. Campaigns are too short and the electorate too absorbed with its own concerns for any political profit to be realized from an evangelical approach.

The most notable example of a candidate ignoring poll results in recent elections is Barry Goldwater in 1964. It is not clear whether his consistent espousal of conservative doctrine was an attempt to rally a so-called "hidden" majority to his cause or whether he was determined not to sacrifice his beliefs for political expediency. To a lesser extent, McGovern chose the same path in 1972 with his appeals to the young and the disadvantaged, whom he hoped would vote in uncharacteristic numbers. The results of the 1964 and 1972 elections speak for themselves on the wisdom of this strategy.

Polls are also helpful in highlighting voter perceptions of the candidate. Louis Harris writes of the problem facing John Kennedy in the closing days of the 1960 campaign:

> John Kennedy was shown to be slipping in the final ten days of the 1960 campaign, after picking up a clear lead as a result of the first debate with Richard Nixon. The signs were unmistakable in his late slippage. Anti-Catholic feeling among white Protestants was mounting again and Catholics had become overconfident of his impending victory, so that the more affluent among his coreligionists could feel the luxury of voting their higher income self-interest and/or their conservative political philosophy and desert Kennedy.[13]

The above passage illustrates both strengths and weaknesses of polls. The knowledge that Nixon was gaining among white Protestants and upper-class Catholics provided Kennedy with information on which to base his strategy late in the campaign; he chose to ignore the religious issue and won by a narrow margin. Without polls he could not have had the information that his candidacy was in trouble. Harris's comments concerning the "clear lead" that Kennedy gained as a result of the TV debates with Nixon reveal an inherent weakness in public opinion polls: Intense opinion will be more stable than opinion lightly held. It is difficult to establish gradations of opinion intensity under any conditions, but it is impossible in regard to questions as to candidate preference during election campaigns. The favorable impression Kennedy created through the debates gained some short-term poll support from some voters who had previously intended to vote for Nixon, but this opinion was not of sufficient intensity to be durable. Opinion which is "actionable" is most reliable. Voting is "action" and the closer to Election Day polls are taken the more accurately they will portray the intentions of voters who are polled. The problem of intensity must be understood and taken into consideration by campaign strategists, or the candidate is likely to overrespond to every change in public opinion as measured by the polls.

Another important use of polls is to identify areas of strength and weakness. Elections usually revolve around those states with the largest blocs of electoral college votes — New York, New Jersey, Pennsylvania, Illinois, Ohio, California and Texas. Candidates must spend their time in those states that are doubtful. There is no gain in expending campaign energies in an effort to "lose by less" in states where a candidate is weakest or to win big in "sure" states. Nixon's loss in 1960 is attributed by some to his decision to campaign in Alaska to redeem his pledge of visiting all 50 states rather than spending the last campaign days in Illinois, which he lost by a narrow margin.

CAMPAIGN FINANCING

The cost of Presidential campaigns has escalated dramatically with the shift away from person-to-person party-dominated

TABLE 7–3

ELECTION CAMPAIGN COSTS FOR NATIONAL OFFICES, 1960–68

	1960	1964	1968
Campaign costs	$32,896,000	$47,763,000	$69,999,000
National spending	$28,074,000	$38,601,000	$62,765,000
Democrats	42.0%	34.6%	21.6%
Republicans	46.1%	50.0%	46.9%
Wallace	—	—	11.5%
Labor committees	8.7%	9.9%	12.2%

Note: Covers expenditures officially reported to the Clerk of the House and the Secretary of the Senate. Cost of political activity at all levels, including primaries and intrastate committees, estimated by Citizens' Research Foundation at $200 million for 1964 and $300 million for 1968. Known campaign debts not actually reported were added to reported expenditures to determine total spending. Remaining expenditures by national committees not reported in the table are accounted for by miscellaneous groups.

Source: Statistical Abstract of the United States, 1973, No. 617, p. 383.

efforts and toward mass-media efforts. The Republican Party spent $100,000 to elect Abraham Lincoln in 1860; 100 years later that sum would buy only one half hour of network television.[14] Table 7–3 illustrates the tremendous increase in overall campaign costs in the 1960–68 period.

As Table 7-3 reveals, a substantial percentage of political funds raised in Presidential years goes to the Presidential campaign. Failure to include intrastate committee expenditure drastically diminishes the amount reported; for instance, less than 25 percent of the money spent in 1968 was actually reported under the law.

The Federal Election Campaign Act of 1971, designed to force disclosure of uses and sources of campaign funds, became effective April 1, 1972. Committees must report periodically before an election giving names, addresses, and occupations of those contributing over $100. Obviously, a contributor wishing to remain anonymous can do so by giving no more than $100 to as many committees as he wishes. It has been noted that this would take some bookkeeping adjustments, "but the parties to campaign financing have previously shown little reluctance to do the necessary bookkeeping when it was necessary to get around inconvenient provisions."[16]

Legislation has been proposed to strictly limit contributions of individuals by controlling the number of committees. The 1972 fund-raising effort of the Committee to Reelect the President (estimated at about 70 million) offered proof that the 1971 law was inadequate. This law also attempted to control spending for mass media, but this did not prevent expenditures from reaching new highs.

The question of campaign spending is complex. A candidate challenging an incumbent might be severely handicapped if stringent spending restrictions were imposed. The President has access to media coverage daily and can make innumerable "nonpolitical" speeches and appearances in the course of a campaign. This exposure is difficult for a challenger to match or overcome under the best of circumstances but impossible if spending is limited drastically. A possible solution to this quandary would be to shorten the campaign to about one month and limit the amount of radio and television available to the candidates. A shortened campaign would reduce the funds necessary and make possible some limitation of the use of the media by the President for political purposes.

Financing Presidential election campaigns is one of the most important tasks of the organization. It is also the area in which we observe the greatest abuses of the Democratic process. Stories of ambassadorships, Cabinet appointments and federal judgeships being promised in return for contributions follow every election. As the need for money has increased, the abuses have kept pace. Personal solicitations are the standard approach for large contributions, while increasing use has been made of direct mail to solicit smaller gifts.

NEW CAMPAIGN SPENDING LEGISLATION

A new campaign spending bill was passed in October, 1974.

which is intended to limit the political influence of special interest groups and wealthy individuals. This legislation limits spending in Presidential primaries to $10 million plus $2 million for fund-raising activities. A limit of $20 million was imposed for Presidential election campaigns. These funds will be partly provided by the government. Private contributions of $250 or less will be matched by federal monies up to a limit of $5 million. Limits are also placed on individual contributions. No individual can contribute more than $25,000 to all federal candidates and campaign organizations in an election year.

The strategy employed in Presidential election contests is simply a reflection of contemporary political realities and social values. The decrease of the role of party is recognition that its power to deliver the vote – if it ever existed to the extent credited – has diminished. The emphasis on television rises from the fact that this is the medium most Americans turn to for their political news.

The most significant social development is that increased cynicism toward our social and political institutions has made rationalization easy for those who have circumvented election laws. As Presidential power has increased over the past two decades, more power has accrued to those closest to the oval office. Since campaign aides venture forth in the reflected power and glory of their leader, is it any wonder the "zealots for Nixon" set a new high in campaign abuses and a new low in political morality? The oft-quoted turn-of-the-century words of Lord Acton offer a succinct explanation of illegality in Presidential campaigns: "Power tends to corrupt and absolute power corrupts absolutely."

NOTES

1. Robert Agronoff, ed., *The New Style in Election Campaigns* (Boston: Holbrook Press, 1972), pp. 5-6. Also see Frank Sorauf, *Political Parties in the American System* (Boston: Little, Brown & Co., 1964) pp. 108-13.

2. Robert Agronoff, "Role of Political Parties in the New Campaigning," in *The New Style in Election Campaigns*, p. 98.

3. Melvyn Bloom, *Public Relations and Presidential Campaigns* (New York: Thomas Y. Crowell Co., 1973), p. 26.

4. Stanley Kelley, Jr., *Professional Public Relations and Political Power* (Baltimore: Johns Hopkins Press, 1956), p. 151.

5. Bloom, *Public Relations and Presidential Campaigns*, p. 63.

6. From *Subverse: Rhymes for Our Times* by Marya Mannes and Robert Osborn (New York: George Braziller, Inc., 1959), as quoted in Walter Troy Spencer, "The Agency Knack of Political Packaging," in Robert Agronoff, ed., *The New Style in Election Campaigns*, p. 78.

7. Bloom, *Public Relations and Presidential Campaigns*, p. 211.

8. A detailed discussion of Nixon's campaign appears in Joe McGinniss's *The Selling of the President 1968* (New York: Trident Press, 1969).

9. Quoted in Bloom, *Public Relations and Presidential Campaigns*, p. 229.

10. Ibid., p. 284.

11. Thomas W. Benham, "Polling for a Presidential Candidate," in Robert Agronoff, ed., *The New Style in Election Campaigns*, p. 214.

12. Charles W. Roll, Jr., and Albert H. Cantrill, *Polls* (New York: Basic Books, 1972), p. 36. Other excellent works on the use of polls in campaigns are Harold Mendelsohn and Irving Crespi, *Polls, Television and the New Politics* (Scranton, Pa.: Chandler Publishing Co., 1970), and Leo Bogart, *Silent Politics: Polls and the Awareness of Public Opinion* (New York: John Wiley & Sons, 1972).

13. Louis Harris, *The Anguish of Change* (New York: W. W. Norton & Co., 1973), p. 24.

14. Hugh A. Bone, *American Politics and the Party System*, 4th Edn. (New York: McGraw-Hill Book Co., 1971), p. 391.

15. David Nichols, *Financing Elections* (New York: New Viewpoints, 1974), p. 147.

8 Elections In Perspective

Each Presidential election has a certain unique quality. Politics and the society within which it flourishes are in a constant state of flux; as societal values and priorities change, so does the political environment. The four-year period between Presidential elections is sufficient for some issues to fade and others to appear. When the new priorities are markedly different from the old, it may presage a change in political alignment that will endure over the span of several elections.

Candidates for the Presidency must campaign within a political ebb and flow that is largely outside their control. In the case of an incumbent running for reelection, the election assumes the nature of a vote of confidence in the administration. The challenger is more dependent upon dissatisfaction with the incumbent than upon his own political platform. It has been pointed out that the advantage accruing to an incumbent seeking reelection can hardly be exaggerated. While the President cannot control all political, social, or economic events, he has an opportunity to interpret their significance in a manner which puts his administration in a favorable light.

THE PAST FOUR DECADES

Table 8-1 yields interesting insights into the nature of Presidential elections. In no instance in the 11 elections included in this table did an incumbent President fail to win reelection if he ran for another term. What the data demonstrates about our political system in general and the Presidency in particular is the stability and viability of the two-party system over the past 40 years. Note that the lowest percentage for a losing candidate was 36.5 percent in 1936, and the highest percentage of the popular vote was Lyndon Johnson's 61.1 percent in 1964. While we are accustomed to speak of landslides in elections of this kind, the remarkable fact is that no President has been able to garner much over 60 percent of the popular vote. Consider this in light of the events taking place when these elections were held. Franklin Roosevelt had captured the imagination of much of the country with his legislative avalanche at a time of great economic depression. The entire concept of the federal government was changed, from an institution doing only what states or local government could not do for the citizenry to an aggressive institution seeking to impose federal dominance on virtually every facet of the nation's economic and social life. Despite this significant change, Roosevelt increased his share of the popular vote by little more than 3 percent. This gives rise to two ideas. First, there was obviously no real consensus on the desirability of what was then considered radical legislation. Second, despite the lack of strength of the Republican Party in 1936 and the limited appeal of Alfred M. Landon, there was a residual opposition of almost 40 percent that opposed the incumbent.

The nature of this apparently stable opposition in American politics is widely misunderstood. It is usually attributed to consistent party strength, but the data in this book demonstrate the fraility of such assertions. A more plausible explanation, it seems, is that pluralism in American society dictates that there will always be competing interests in political and social spheres. The resolution of these differences leads to a sizable minority that will vote against the incumbent regardless of how poorly the challenging party is organized or how weak its candidate. This reservoir of opposition, then, may be attributed to the nature of our pluralistic society rather than to enduring political bonds.

The sweeping changes of the Roosevelt years did bring about a basic realignment in party coalitions. This is concealed by the data in Table 8-1, which show that Roosevelt garnered between 53.4 and 60.8 percent of the popular vote in his four victories. Within these electoral majorities there were basic changes that served to establish the Democrats as the working man's party and the Republicans as the party of the wealthy and privileged. Thus a Democratic coalition was formed which included the traditionally Democratic Solid South and urban areas in all parts of the country and which dominated Presidential politics until 1952. This 20-year period of Democratic control of the White House—roughly one generation—was forged initially from the despair of depression and was maintained by the imperatives of

TABLE 8-1

POPULAR VOTE IN PRESIDENTIAL ELECTIONS, 1932-72

Year	Candidates		Percentage of Popular Vote	
	Democratic	Republican	Democrat	Republican
1932	Franklin D. Roosevelt	Herbert C. Hoover	57.4%	39.6%
1936	Franklin D. Roosevelt	Alfred M. Landon	60.8	36.5
1940	Franklin D. Roosevelt	Wendell L. Willkie	54.7	44.8
1944	Franklin D. Roosevelt	Thomas E. Dewey	53.4	45.9
1948	Harry S. Truman	Thomas E. Dewey	49.6	45.1
1952	Adlai E. Stevenson	Dwight D. Eisenhower	44.4	55.1
1956	Adlai E. Stevenson	Dwight D. Eisenhower	42.0	57.4
1960	John F. Kennedy	Richard M. Nixon	49.5	49.3
1964	Lyndon B. Johnson	Barry Goldwater	61.1	38.5
1968	Hubert H. Humphrey	Richard M. Nixon	42.7	43.4
1972	George C. McGovern	Richard M. Nixon	37.5	60.7

Source: *Statistical Abstract of the United States, 1973*, No. 590, p. 364.

World War II and the feeling that national leadership should remain constant during war.

It is likely that the victories of Dwight Eisenhower in 1952 and 1956 represented something more than affection for a war hero. They also presaged the beginning of the end of Democratic domination of the South. This is probably attributable to the beginnings of a broad-based conservative reaction to the New Deal years which first manifested itself in a notably conservative region. The emergence of the southern Negro as a political force – pro-Democratic – also contributed heavily. The ease with which Eisenhower won reelection in 1956 and Johnson won in 1964 gives further evidence of the advantage accruing to an incumbent President. The retention of an administration is associated with stability, and the prospect of "business as usual" seems to be most appealing to the largest percentage of the electorate. The only exception to this in the period under discussion was in 1932, when economic crisis made the promise of drastic Presidential action acceptable. Richard Nixon's victory in 1972 over a challenger who called for change is a reaffirmation of this principle.

ALTERNATION IN POWER

How, then, do we explain the alternation in Presidential power over the past 40 years? After eight years in office, any President has accumulated blame for a multitude of problems that have refused to disappear during his tenure. Since electing his successor involves change, the challenger has an opportunity to offer alternatives to administration policy without running against the innate desire for stability that he would have to surmount in facing an incumbent. Both parties attempt to sit astride the political "center" in an effort to win. Occasionally, candidates misread or ignore the public mood, and landslide victories for their opponents result. The dimensions of Barry Goldwater's defeat in 1964 and that of George McGovern in 1972 resulted from this failure to properly assess the public mood. It is unlikely that either would have won regardless of the positions taken, as they were both challenging incumbents, but it is probable that the elections would have been much closer. There have been only three elections in the past 40 years — 1952, 1960, and 1968 — in which there was no incumbent running for reelection. In each instance the election resulted in a change of party rule.

Even if the incumbent party is successful in electing its candidate, the election will probably be very close. In 1960 and 1968 the incumbent party lost the elections by very narrow margins. There has been no instance in the past 40 years of a President running for reelection after one term and losing. It is conceivable that this might occur if the nation suffered severe economic setbacks. In reality, however, the incumbent is able to keep the economy reasonably vibrant through pump-priming for at least the first term. Nixon's economic policies reflect this situation. He assumed office amid rising inflation and unemployment. For the first two years of his administration, economic policy was guided by a determination to reduce the rate of inflation despite an attendant rise in unemployment. When this policy failed, wage and price controls (thoroughly un-Republican) were imposed, and large budget deficits were incurred as more money was pumped into the economy. This policy, a short-term effort to improve the economic picture, succeeded, and Nixon was reelected handily. If it had failed the election would have probably been very close.

A basic equilibrium in the political arena is maintained by competing interests. Virtually all legislation benefits one segment of society at the expense of others. For instance, increases in federal taxes may be welcomed by some if they are to benefit from new government programs. Taxpayers who do not expect to benefit, however, will react with dismay to this dilution of their income. Legislation that fosters school integration will be applauded by some segments in society but opposed by others. It is this natural dichotomy of interests manifesting itself in most government policy decisions that produces the counterforces that ensure competition. The allocation of resources produces conflict, which is the lifeblood of politics.

The Democratic and Republican parties have retained their potential for power because the electorate has not hesitated to use its ballot to achieve a change of party in the White House. V. O. Key, Jr., alludes to the rational behavior of the electorate, which appears to be basically a vote of confidence or no confidence in the incumbent administration rather than a clear-cut choice between the policies advocated by the candidates.[1] This is symptomatic of consensus politics, which is a hallmark of most stable political systems. Consensus is used in the sense of general agreement on desirable ends and in no way implies agreement on means. For example, virtually everyone will agree that all the nation's children should be provided a quality education. When busing is suggested as one means to accomplish this, however, disagreements arise.

Presidential elections, then, cannot be equated with referendums on specific questions. In 1968 an alternative to the Republican and Democratic parties was injected into the contest in the person of George Wallace. The Wallace vote is best viewed as a protest against the social policies of both major parties. Although Wallace offered only broad generalities as policy positions, his campaign appeared directed at a "white backlash." Those who voted for him knew he could not win; their votes were a manifestation of discontent, or votes of no-confidence in either the Republicans or the Democrats.

THE CRISIS OF LEGITIMACY

Society today is experiencing a crisis of legitimacy which pervades the political and social life of the nation. The manifestations of this crisis are many and diverse, but the result is the same in every case. We are witnessing increasing skepticism about the viability of social and political institutions which have served as wellsprings of confidence in the past. Racial conflict is only the tip of the iceberg; blacks are not the only group questioning the legitimacy of prevailing institutions.

Table 8-2 points to the diminished confidence in political institutions, the media, and groups in society who traditionally

TABLE 8-2

INDEX OF PUBLIC TRUST IN U.S. INSTITUTIONS

Great Deal of Confidence in:	1972	1971	1966
Medicine	48%	61%	72%c
Finance	39	36	67
Science	37	32	56
Military	35	27	62
Education	33	37	61
Psychiatry	31	35	51
Religion	30	27	41
Retail business	28	24	48
U. S. Supreme Court	28	23	51
Federal executive branch	27	23	41
Major U.S. companies	27	27	55
Congress	21	19	42
The press	18	18	29
Television	17	22	25
Labor	15	14	22
Advertising	12	13	21

Source: Harris Survey. Chicago Tribune–New York News Syndicate, Inc., October 25, 1971; Harris Survey, *The Philadelphia Inquirer*, November 13, 1972.

have been among the most respected. For three years between 1966 and 1972, a nationwide cross section was asked: "As far as people running these institutions are concerned, would you say you have a great deal of confidence, only some confidence, or hardly any confidence at all in them?"

The erosion of public trust seen in Table 8-2 may be attributed to many causes. One of the most pertinent is the steadily rising level of education and income, which has meant that more Americans form their own judgments of political and societal institutions. Rising income also leads to increased feelings of efficacy in the individual's position vis-à-vis the environment. The decreased legitimacy of our institutions is dealt with extensively in *The Hidden Crisis in American Politics* by Samuel

Lubell.[2] He notes that it is the function of government to arbitrate the clashes between conflicting expectations, and it is the public's assessment of the fairness of these arbitrations that determines the status of government in the eyes of the citizenry. Lubell suggests:

> Perhaps we need to drop the pretense that government is a substitute for God, and face up to the real crisis of authority, which is that of self-government. There are no gods among us; only men who must learn to govern themselves.
>
> If that is so, a large part of our crisis is the need to make government believable. Can that be done in times like these, with so much unreconciled conflict, a war not ended, such clashing expectations, spreading distrusts?
>
> The blunt fact is that the old formulas that we took for granted have been lost, and we now must consciously determine what mixture of fear and hope, restraint and freedom, competition and subsidy, the market or priorities, will gain public trust. At some point there may be too much government; at other points we may have to test new governmental mechanisms.[3]

Lubell interprets the changing values of society in political terms and considers loss of confidence in the government as the focal point of the cynicism. One might argue that it is the breakdown in traditional touchstones in society—the family, church, and so on—that is the cause of the political legitimacy crisis. Whichever approach one prefers, it is apparent that we are witnessing a reordering of social and political values.

Despite the evidence in this chapter that there is an increasing lack of public confidence in government, the electorate shies away from a candidate who represents change. It can be hypothesized that the legitimacy crisis in the nation is real, but neither party appears capable of inspiring change. Public displeasure is not of sufficient force to encourage pursuit of drastic political solutions to the nation's problems.

The root of our societal and political problems, according to Lubell, is "the ceaseless struggle for national unification, in our constant striving for 'that more perfect union.' This has always been a distinctively American problem because of our immense geographical expanse and the astonishing variety of people drawn to our shores."[4] Perhaps the idea that it is "normal" to have one dominant political party has its origins in the drive for national unity to which Lubell alludes. The notion of a two-party system with one party dominant is ingrained in political writings of the past 40 years. At the same time, the lack of underlying party loyalty and the resultant dramatic shifts in voting behavior observed over the past 20 years bear testimony to the changed nature of American politics. Whether this change is a temporary phenomenon or a permanent restructuring of our national political life is uncertain. Nor can we be sure that it is desirable to have a national party in long-term dominance, with a minority party capable only of challenging weakly except in unusual circumstances. If a minority can effectively compete for the Presidency only on rare occasions, it ceases to be a potent political force. It might be completely workable in our political system to have two major parties competing for the Presidency, with an eight-year pattern of alternation. This schema would suggest little party loyalty and basic national agreement on the ends toward which society should strive.

Lubell interprets these changes in the nature of American politics as reaction by the electorate to the ever-increasing scope of federal power. The political shifts of the past 20 years are viewed as an attempt by the voters to protect themselves against this increased governmental control. He sees the trend toward the use of both parties as being fed by numerous changes in American life:

> ... better education; the weakening of the hometown tradition as millions of families moved from one part of the country to another; the declining importance of religion in shaping people's vote; the growth of industry in so many sections of the country. Because of these and other changes, different parts of the nation have become ever more alike, and have tended to shift together.[5]

These changes to which Lubell refers go far in explaining the legitimacy crisis. With values in a state of flux, it is natural that those institutions which have become symbols of stability should be among the first challenged by the new values.

PARTIES AND THE PRESIDENCY

Students of American political parties have long lamented the fractionated nature of the party system. It is believed that this diffusion of political power renders the parties incapable of cohesive action and therefore impotent in the face of manifold problems. James MacGregor Burns properly notes that a multiplicity of power centers have arisen from our decentralized political framework, each with its own constituency.[6] Burns concludes that "The paramount fact about American political parties is their organizational weakness at all levels, from local to national."[7] The increase in split-ticket voting and the domination of party organizations by the candidates give evidence of the validity of Burns's observations.

Barring ideological schisms of far greater magnitude than we observe at this time, it is likely that both parties will straddle the political center (although it will shift) and make their greatest effort to regain power when an incumbent cannot succeed himself.

There is no doubt that political party organizations have lost much of their influence. The advent of the civil service and the accompanying decrease in the number of jobs which could be handed out as political patronage deprived the parties of perhaps their most potent weapon in their quest for loyalty. Even among prospective candidates, the incentives for loyalty are few. If a candidate can raise enough money, he can mount his campaign without the need to spend years in the party hierarchy proving his worth. Television, of course, has had a dramatic impact on political campaigning. A well-financed candidate can transfer himself from a virtual unknown to a recognized public figure largely through television exposure. Needless to say, the candidate who finances his own campaign and wins does not feel beholden to the organization. Since most political contributions go to committees sponsoring a given candidate rather than directly to party coffers, a candidate who must rely on his party for financing is in trouble. National party organizations are, in reality, Presidential parties.

The decline of political parties as touchstones for our political values has occurred in tandem with the decline of party loyalty by the individual. It is difficult to envisage circumstances in the near future that will enable the national parties to regain their hegemony over party affairs, although they do retain the potential to serve as rallying points. Barring a widening ideological gap between the Democratic and Republican parties, however, this potential will probably be unrealized. There are interest groups of sufficient power and influence to be heard in governmental councils without the need for such an intermediary as a political party. It is unlikely that groups with power will voluntarily relinquish their influence. It could be argued that interest groups are actually superior to parties as a channel through which individuals may make demands upon government. They have the virtue of representing people with shared interests, albeit on a narrow range of issues. Political parties have survived by attempting to encompass the broadest possible spectrum of public opinion.

The growth of the nation and the increased complexity of its problems have led to government by technocrats. This evolution from government through elected representatives to government by a bureaucracy that survives regardless of electoral outcome marks a diminution of the concept of participatory democracy. The electorate still has a choice, to to sure, but the choice is limited to selecting leaders rather than choosing from clearly defined policy alternatives.

What, then, is the future of American political parties? It is highly unlikely that they will be relegated permanently to a position subservient to that of interest groups. Party politics will play a role in response to the demands of the times, a view that places the emphasis on their reactive capabilities as opposed to an innovative role. Theodore Lowi refers to this as the "politics of dead center":

> Centricity prevails, first of all, because the candidates give the voters no choice but centricity. Even if the polls did not tilt the responses in favor of moderation, the candidates would. They hang together so closely around a mean that voters must vote for a middle-of-the-road position or stay home.[8]

Just as political candidates seek the attitudinal center, so do parties become agents for preserving the system rather than initiating change. If change comes through other channels, the parties adjust their positions to accommodate the new conditions. The Supreme Court school desegregation decision in 1954 was a pivotal moment in the struggle for racial equality. The parties responded to this change, but they would have been incapable of precipitating it because of their inherent conservatism. Stability, then, is the trait the parties represent. Curiously, though, it is this stability that has led increasing numbers of voters to cross party lines. The politics of the status quo reduces electoral choice to a judgment of the incumbent. Voters ensure change in leadership by their electoral behavior, which mirrors the feeling that it is wise to stay with an incumbent but better to change parties if no incumbent is running. This may be attributed to cynicism about government corruption and the belief that change helps prevent moral and ethical laxity.

If the parties are agents of stability and this tends to erode their influence, under what circumstances will they become dominant? In a period of social change to which the political system is unable to respond, the electorate will demand positive political action. This is a task that the political parties retain a potential to accomplish in our system. In any period of change, there will be those who are inclined toward the preservation of the status quo, a situation which produces two-party electoral competition at its best. Since fundamental issues cannot be resolved during the course of one administration, party loyalty will increase as the issues take on an ideological hue. This was the experience following Roosevelt's victory in 1932; only after the ideological question concerning the role of government in everyday economic and social life was resolved did party loyalty wane and a period of party alternation commence in the White House.

At present, there are no issues which appear to arouse a sizable segment of the electorate. Presidential elections have been reduced to votes of confidence in the incumbent administration. Party loyalty, therefore, has declined because of the absence of issues that are salient and on which the parties can take markedly different positions. We can expect this loyalty to reemerge under the same conditions that will cause a resurgence in political party strength.

The higher level of political knowledge possessed by today's voter makes him prone to independency unless circumstances dictate otherwise. There is nothing "natural" about party loyalty, any more than parties are the "natural" arbiters of political opinion. Institutions in a democratic society arise through necessity. When the need dissipates, the institutions wither. In a similar manner, party loyalty is an outgrowth of the voter's acceptance of the party as a political reference point. Party loyalty of the future will be based on its potential to bring about change which the individual voter desires and which the opposing party does not favor. Thus, party loyalty may develop for different reasons than it has in the past.

The potential for ideological conflict certainly exists in American society. Within the Democratic and Republican parties there are sharply divergent views on the proper goals for society and the order of priorities. These ideological considerations are usually muted because of the necessity of attracting broad-based electoral support. Social or economic upheaval, however, might unleash these forces and draw recognizable lines of demarcation between the policy positions of the two major parties. This condition will not only bring about a rise in party loyalty but will probably reverse the trend toward steadily lower percentages voting in Presidential elections. The same fervor that inspires loyalty will inspire people to exercise their franchise.

The future of both political parties and voting behavior is a function of the social and political environment that ensues. Neither move in a unidirectional, nonreversible way. Both the individual voter and the parties that seek his support respond to the exigencies of any given period. It is likely that the period of party weakness and voter antipathy to parties that we have witnessed in the past two decades will endure until a crisis develops of the magnitude that the nation faced in 1932. An ideological interpretation of events by both parties and voters rallying to the party best expressing their views can then be expected. Change is the constant in American politics, and any analysis of either parties or voting behavior will fail if this fact is not given proper weight.

NOTES

1. V. O. Key, Jr., with Milton C. Cummings, *The Responsible Electorate* (New York: Vintage Books, 1968), p. 7.

2. Samuel Lubell, *The Hidden Crisis in American Politics* (New York: W. W. Norton & Co., 1970).

3. Ibid., p. 297.

4. Ibid., pp. 32–33.

5. Ibid., p. 42.

6. James MacGregor Burns, *The Deadlock of Democracy* (Englewood Cliffs, N. J.: Prentice-Hall, 1963), p. 205.

7. Ibid., p. 236.

8. Theodore Lowi, "The Artificial Majority," *The Nation*, December 7, 1970.

9 Conclusions

We are in an era of consensus politics in which the Republican and Democratic parties are offering philosophic differences rather than programmatic alternatives. As long as this situation exists we are likely to witness a continuation of candidate-dominated national political parties, a brand of politics often criticized on the grounds that it does not offer the electorate a viable choice. The elections surveyed in this book do not substantiate that pessimistic view. An increasingly well-informed, increasingly middle-class electorate has not hesitated to visit electoral defeat on administrations that do not meet with their approval.

The American right to vote for a national leader every four years forms a bond between the ruler and the ruled.[1] A President can be reelected only if he has avoided antagonizing a majority of voters, and the voters know that the President they elect will serve four years, barring death, impeachment, or resignation. Presidential elections thus provide a periodic review of government by the citizenry.

It is reassuring to observe that contemporary American

society is not compliant, willing to simply observe the machinations of their leaders. The Watergate affair has brought the legitimacy of government into question. It represents an abuse of power by those closest to the President and by the Chief Executive. The fact that this story could not be quashed is tangible proof of the viability of the political system. The President is the most powerful official in the land, but he is not all-powerful. He is subject to scrutiny by the media, the bureaucracy, Congress, and the judiciary. All have played a role in preventing a Watergate cover-up.

Voters' Decisions

Voters are not well informed if measured by responses to public opinion polls on specific policy questions. But elections since 1952 indicate that they are capable of expressing their displeasure with the course of government on Election day. This is not an irrational reaction to high-powered media campaigns. The books that have appeared in the past few years suggesting that Presidential races are really glorified competition between advertising agencies make amusing reading but poor political science.

A brief look at elections since 1952 will demonstrate the inherent wisdom of a mass electorate. Almost 20 years of war and depression will tax even the most stalwart of people. Dwight Eisenhower was a war hero, and he did have a father image and an engaging smile. But none of these attributes can explain his victory. In 1952 the American electorate displayed their unhappiness with the Korean War and severe labor problems and vented their feelings at the expense of the Democratic candidate. Adlai Stevenson did not lose because he was an "egghead." He was an eminently respectable candidate who had the misfortune to run in a year when the Democrats had little or no chance for success. The 1956 election followed four years of relative tranquility marked by a manageable recession and no war. It was the first four years since the 1920s when the nation enjoyed a degree of quietude. Eisenhower was reelected because he had avoided offending too many voters. His style was too passive for many but not to a sufficiently large segment of the electorate that they would elect Stevenson in his stead.

The 1960 election illustrates the situation in which an incumbent has served eight years and leaves office with considerable public esteem. Eisenhower is one of the few Presidents in this century who have managed this feat. This made John Kennedy's task a difficult one, compounded by the uncertain impact of the religious issue. He was aided materially by his youth and vigor, which contrasted favorably with the older Eisenhower. The campaign captured the public imagination but represented neither a resounding vote of confidence in Kennedy nor a rejection of Richard Nixon.

Lyndon Johnson had widespread approval of his performance in office after the assassination of John Kennedy. The economy was booming, and the Republicans had no chance in 1964. Barry Goldwater's campaign increased the margin of Johnson's victory, but it did offer a valuable lesson to all willing to learn. Doctrinaire politics are not palatable to the overwhelming majority of the American electorate. The demise of Johnson's public standing at the end of this term was so dramatic and so intense that much of the voters' approbation was directed at him personally, not at the party. Nixon's election in 1968 was almost as close as his defeat in 1960. The candidacy of George Wallace probably did more to hold his margin of victory down than did the opposition of Hubert Humphrey. The 1968 election took place in a year of racial ferment, campus disruption, and war weariness. In a two-party race, the Democrats had little opportunity. The 1972 election again demonstrated the inherent advantage in incumbency and the folly of appeals to a small segment of the electorate. A moderate Democratic candidate would probably have fared better than George McGovern did.

Party Alternation

There is nothing in the Presidential races since 1952 to suggest an irrational or poorly informed electorate. Nor is there any evidence that voters are as influenced by party as is popularly supposed. Presidential politics of the past 20 years has had a certain rhythm which has alternated between activist and more passive approaches to government. Detente aside, Nixon's policies were more concerned with the status quo than with social engineering. What lies ahead? The resignation of Nixon adds a new dimension to the 1976 election. The completion of Gerald Ford's first term marks the end of 8 years of Republican control of the White House. The chances for Republican success lie in Ford's ability to separate his administration in the public's view from the Nixon scandals. If the electorate perceives of Ford's term as simply an extension of the Nixon years it is likely that the pattern of eight year alternative will continue with a Democratic victory.

The Nature of Presidential Elections

American elections do not provide the type of referendum that parliamentary systems do. The President is elected independently of Congress, and the policy outcome of an election is unclear. The significance of Presidential elections is often challenged on this point. Candidates tend to mute their differences during the campaign, so that we vote with no clear knowledge of what they will do if elected.

Candidates who win by large margins like to view their victories as mandates, but this is an exaggerated interpretation. Elections can only be mandates if both candidates articulate specific positions and legislative proposals on a variety of issues and have the ability to turn these into law. When Presidents ascend to office, the opposition often has a Congressional majority. The power to implement programs in the wake of electoral success is further clouded by the limited control a President has over members of his own party. A convincing argument can be made that elections are not intended as legislative mandates. Voters may be influenced by their perceptions of a candidate's stand on issues they view as salient but totally disagree with other less relevant positions.[2]

Despite the lack of the mandate characteristic in American Presidential elections, they do serve the primary purpose of ensuring the responsiveness of government to the electorate. Public opinion is a mighty force in controlling the actions of any President and protecting the nation against excesses. A President will usually test the water of public opinion before embarking on a new course, and the desire to be reelected is of paramount importance to him in his first term. The need to control the bureaucracy and retain influence in Congress assures second-term responsiveness. The legal machinations during the Watergate hearings illustrate this fact. The President's reluctance to be forthcoming would have been difficult for the courts and Congress to challenge but for the overwhelming tide of opinion expressing disapproval of these maneuvers. This public demonstration of opinion emboldened Congress to insist on its prerogatives and led to Nixon's resignation.

Election issues are seldom specific. If the energy problem is salient to the electorate in 1976, the debate will center around which candidate is best equipped to handle it rather than the specifics of how to do so. In this context, elections represent mandates to get the job done, with the means left to the judgment of the President. It is the lack of specificity of issues that has placed emphasis on the personal appeal of the candidate, with the appearance of competence the most important personality trait. The electorate is not composed of fools. If a candidate combines an aura of competence plus charisma, so much the better. The election thus represents a personal mandate to a candidate adjudged competent to serve the best interests of the nation. By the same token, he is not given carte blanche by the voters; it is assumed that he will act responsibly.

The rapid pace of social change is exemplified by increasing demands for political participation by many segments of the electorate. Even the clergy has demonstrated a penchant for political activity. Much of this thrust is directed at centers of influence—legislators, bureaucrats, and so on—rather than at parties. The Democratic Party has attempted to diffuse and organize some of this activism within its ranks by opening the organization to those who have been underrepresented, but the conflict at the 1972 convention makes it probable that this effort at participatory democracy will be muted in the future.

Parties are not being abandoned by the electorate. They are, however, no longer the prime channel for transmitting demands to the government. Activists use the party machinery selectively but have no qualms about bypassing it if another route appears more effective. Samuel Lubell notes that most voters in the last generation seemed to feel they could best protect their political interests by sticking to one party:

> In the five presidential elections from 1932 through 1948, just over half—51 percent—of the counties in the country, including nearly all of the most populous cities, and many of their suburbs, cast a majority of their vote for the same party's presidential candidate each time.
>
> But in the five elections that followed, spanning 1952 through 1968, only a fifth—22 percent—of the counties stuck with the same party's nominees.[3]

Approaching 1976

We have discussed the changes taking place in the nature of the individual elector and the political party organizations through which the vote is transmitted. Now we will turn our attention to the future. The emphasis is not on prediction but on understanding our political and social environment and the implication for changes in the perceptions of the individual and the role of the party.

The nation is in the midst of rapid social change. The past 30 years have seen a population growth of over 50 percent, with a sharp increase in the number of citizens under 30 years old. We have also witnessed a migration from rural areas to the cities. The social impact of these qualitative and quantitative changes can hardly be exaggerated. The viability of political institutions is tested by their ability to meet new demands. At the same time, there is a need for political institutions to anticipate social demands rather than simply responding to them.[4] An imbalance between the capabilities of the political system to adjust to and to influence social systems creates the type of legitimacy crisis we are experiencing. The failure of political parties to meet societal needs is not entirely due to structural flaws in the system. Rather, political institutions are dependent on popular support if they are to assume new or more active roles. This sentiment has not yet become evident in this country and the national parties will be unable to dominate the political scene until events dictate the preeminence of the parties.

The prospects for modernization of the party system are largely dependent on legislation that would encourage party centralization. This could be achieved in large measure through appropriate legislation. If campaign funds were channeled through the party instead of through individuals, the process of party dominance would be accelerated. This is, of course, a legislative matter. Since the power of the individual Congressman or even President would be curtailed by financial dependence on the party coffers, this type of legislation will not be enacted until there is a popular demand for it. The excesses in campaign spending have received increasing attention, and curtailment could involve centralized fund-raising. Strong, unified parties could articulate their programs in a cohesive manner. In this way the electorate would be more apt to "choose sides" and exhibit some degree of party regularity.

Most theorists agree that the parties can play an essential role in the organization of government and the articulation of issues. Walter Dean Burnham indicates his concern for the future of political parties:

> . . . political parties, with all their well-known human and structured shortcomings, are the only devices thus far invented by the wit of Western man that can, with some effectiveness, generate countervailing collective power on behalf of the many individually powerless against the relatively few who are individually or organizationally powerful.[5]

This view undoubtedly expresses the sentiments of most observers. However, the increased influence of interest groups and the decline in party power have altered the relationship between the elector as an individual and the government he seeks to influence.

The increasingly discriminating judgment of the electorate bodes well for the future of American politics. Political parties can no longer automatically depend on their followers for support in Presidential races, nor can a President assume that once elected he will escape the critical eye of the public. The decline in the importance of parties as arbiters of political life has made many observers uneasy. It is easier to understand a political system with fixed reference points than to make order out of the turbulent politics of the past decade. The political system, however, has demonstrated resiliency in the midst of rapid change, if not foresight. Presidential elections cannot, in themselves, assure governments led by men of integrity and wisdom. They do, however, limit the tenure of unresponsive leaders.

NOTES

1. Gerald M. Pomper, *Elections in America* (New York: Dodd, Mead & Co., 1970), p. 246.

2. Nelson W. Polsby and Aaron B. Wildavsky, *Presidential Elections* (New York: Charles Scribner's Sons, 1971), pp. 299–302.

3. Samuel Lubell, *The Hidden Crisis in American Politics* (New York: W. W. Norton Company, Inc., 1970). pp. 41–42.

4. Murray S. Stedman, Jr., "Introduction," in Murray S. Stedman, Jr., ed., *Modernizing American Government* (Englewood Cliffs, N.J.: Prentice-Hall, 1968), pp. 1–9.

5. Walter Dean Burnham, "The End of American Party Politics," in Joseph R. Fiszman and Gene S. Poschman, eds., *The American Political Arena* (Boston: Little, Brown & Co., 1972), p. 257.

Name Index

135

Subject Index